June 2016

P9-CSU-770

To Jane and Bob,

Special Aunt and Uncle,

Loved Godfather,

Caring and giving friends
to Mark and I —

With love and respect,
Pat

NOT JUST A RECIPE
Celebrating People, Places, & Food

Pat Jackman Altomare

BEST RECIPES FROM TEN YEARS
WRITING A NEWSPAPER FOOD COLUMN

INCLUDING SHARED RECIPES
FROM MANY HOME COOKS

ARCHWAY
PUBLISHING

Archway Publishing books may be ordered through booksellers or by contacting:

Archway Publishing
1663 Liberty Drive
Bloomington, IN 47403
www.archwaypublishing.com
1 (888) 242-5904

Because of the dynamic nature of the Internet, any web addresses or links contained in
this book may have changed since publication and may no longer be valid. The views
expressed in this work are solely those of the author and do not necessarily reflect the views
of the publisher, and the publisher hereby disclaims any responsibility for them.

Any people depicted in stock imagery provided by Thinkstock are models,
and such images are being used for illustrative purposes only.
Certain stock imagery © Thinkstock.

ISBN: 978-1-4808-2849-0 (sc)
ISBN: 978-1-4808-2850-6 (e)

Library of Congress Control Number: 2016904177

Print information available on the last page.

Archway Publishing rev. date: 4/15/2016

CONTENTS

Chapter 8   Introduction; Food Gift Ideas

INTRODUCTION

More people than ever are "reading" cookbooks, seeking more information about a recipe, the "who, when, and where" that gives it life. I have poured over my collection of 500- plus past newspaper columns and have chosen recipes that were popular, interesting, and dependable, recipes of home and tradition that have been devoured by food lovers and home cooks who enjoyed them.

NOT JUST A RECIPE is culinary prose containing stories of experiences, family, and travels that came together during my years as a newspaper food columnist, all centered around an infinite variety of recipes. Utilizing a significant human interest component, I present these stories and recipes in a down-to-earth writing style that is relaxed and informal.

It all began in 2003, when I offered a recipe each week to our local paper from a huge collection of recipes I had inherited from Mom, both grandmothers, and Aunts. I started with the best recipes and kept going through the collections that came from these strong women of my past. The recipes had an aura of home, family, and tradition; I couldn't throw them away. They represent years these women spent cooking for their families and how important that was to them. To the recipes I started adding what information I could gather about them. For example, my mother's cinnamon roll-ups were a way to use extra pie dough. I added who made them first and when and how they were named "Just-a-Minute's". The response was overwhelming, interest was piqued as readers learned about my family, life, and travels; always letting me know that they loved *more than just a recipe*. I never lost sight though that the recipes couldn't take a back seat, they had to be good.

I have gathered those recipes and stories that generated a lot of positive feedback and expressions of appreciation, along with thoughtful and enjoyable recollections of events, family, and experiences.

There is a fine line between living in the past and appreciating the past. All I have to do is remember my grandmothers, aunts, and my mother as they were in their kitchens, so much in their element, and it conjures deep feelings of respect and gratitude for their cooking, teachings, and love of family, much of it represented by the recipes they left behind, almost like a signature.

In Chapter five, you will be engaged by delightful home cooks who sent recipes, wrote suggestions, gave feedback and most of all taught me a lot. Meet just a few:

Barbara lives in Australia and introduced me to a Lamington, which is as popular to Aussies as our brownie is to us. Lamingtons are cake squares, chocolate frosted and rolled in coconut, found in bake sales and every convenience store in Australia. Barbara's brother lives in New England and would send my column to her every week, and she would write me of her life in Australia.

Meet Ethyl, originally from Colombia, who graciously shares her family's Hanukah traditions, along with her Colombian variation for Potato Latkes.

And the surprise of meeting Dennis (from Michigan) whose note was in my inbox one morning, concerning a past column I wrote on old cookbooks that focused on the famous Mama Leone's restaurant in New

York. He remembered his mother often making a famous dish from that restaurant, and asked if I could find the recipe.

In NOT JUST A RECIPE you will find a story you identify with, a good recipe that is new to your collection, and more than a few minutes of enjoyment; a cookbook to read that will trigger a memory and bring pleasure.

pja

In Honor of My Mother,
Stella Oles Jackman,
for Her dedication to Family
& Traditions,
and for Being a Great Cook

CHAPTER 1
MOST POPULAR

These recipes and stories generated many e-mails and personal notes from those who followed my newspaper food column; reflecting their enjoyment and pleasure. The recipes are nothing less than special with stories that capture interest and are enjoyable for me to tell.

One recipe is apple-spice wedding cake with cream cheese frosting that was so well-liked at a wedding I attended, that the guests were requesting seconds and thirds if they could get it. The wedding was held in a spectacular setting of an apple orchard in full autumn color, follow along as I share with you this wedding that begins with a beautiful ceremony taking place on a gentle hill overlooking an orchard.

BOWTIE PASTA WITH PROSCIUTTO, PINE NUTS, AND SPINACH
SCALLION BUTTERMILK BISCUITS
SWEET POTATO MINESTRONE WITH TURKEY SAUSAGE
SECOND PLACE BAKED MACARONI & CHEESE
BASIC MARINARA SAUCE
SPINACH AND RICOTTA STUFFED SHELLS
COCONUT CURRY CHICKEN AND SHRIMP SOUP
CARAMEL RHUBARB COBBLER
RHUBARB CUSTARD BARS
WEDDING CAKE; APPLE SPICE WITH CREAM CHEESE FROSTING
CINNAMON ROLL-UPS ("JUST A MINUTES")
STELLA JACKMAN'S NO-FAIL PIE CRUST
JORDAN MARSH BLUEBERRY MUFFINS

BOWTIE PASTA WITH PROSCIUTTO, PINE NUTS, AND SPINACH

This is one of the best pasta dishes my family and I have ever had. No exaggeration. I found it about five years ago when Sara Moulton of the Food Channel, had Vita Greco on as her guest. He is a chef of Italian expertise, and demonstrated how to prepare this pasta dish. It has become a favorite in my collection of recipes. No-one I have ever given this recipe to saw that cooking demonstration, but this has become very popular and is always passed on to more and more people. When a group of friends and I vacationed in a condo in Stow, Vermont, we each took a night to cook a meal of our choice. (The deal was if you shop and cook, you are off clean-up duty); I was certainly up for that deal! I chose to make this pasta recipe on my night to cook as it was quick, without a lot of preparation, and I knew from serving it many times in the past that most everyone would enjoy it.

Some are a little doubtful when they see raisins in a pasta dish, but many have raved about this as soon as they taste it. There's also something a bit special when you use farfalle pasta (bowties); it seems to add a certain pizzazz.

Tip: I use regular spinach and quite a bit more than the recipe calls for.

Also a quality Romano cheese really does top it off with perfection.

INGREDIENTS: *¾ cup pine nuts*
¾ cup raisins (I prefer golden raisins)
½ cup boiling water
½ cup olive oil
4 garlic cloves, minced
1 bag spinach, washed & drained (salad (baby) spinach not flavorful enough for cooking, use regular spinach)

1 pound bowtie pasta (farfalle)
¼ pound prosciutto, sliced into small pieces (can be costly; I have substituted crisply fried bacon or crumbled sweet Italian sausage)
Salt and pepper
Grated Romano cheese

Toast pine nuts in a small frying pan. Add raisins to boiling water till plump, and then drain. In a large frying pan, heat oil and sauté garlic; add spinach and cook until wilted. Cook pasta according to package directions. Drain well and place in a large bowl with the nuts, raisins, spinach mixture, prosciutto, grated cheese, and pepper. Taste, add salt if needed (Prosciutto and cheese are salty). Serve hot.

SCALLION BUTTERMILK BISCUITS

If you live on the West Coast, you call them green onions; on the East Coast, they are scallions. Who knew?

No matter what they are called they are delicious in biscuits.

Serve biscuits at breakfast or dinner.

Try adding different herbs such as fresh chives or fresh dill instead of the scallions.

Preheat oven to 425- degrees.

INGREDIENTS: *4 cups all-purpose flour*
¼ cup sugar
2 tablespoons baking powder
2 teaspoons salt

¾ cup (one and half sticks) cold unsalted butter, cut into
    small pieces
1 and ½ cup cold buttermilk
¼ cup finely chopped scallions
1 large egg, beaten, for glazing

In a large bowl, whisk together first four (dry) ingredients. Add butter and rub it in with your fingertips (or use pastry blender) until mixture resembles coarse meal; add buttermilk and scallions and stir till moist clumps form. Add more buttermilk, 1 tablespoon at a time, if dough is dry.

Divide dough in half. On a floured surface flatten to 3/4 inch thickness. Use a two-inch cookie or biscuit cutter to cut out biscuits. Repeat with remainder of dough. Place on ungreased baking sheets and brush with beaten egg. Bake until golden on top, about 16 minutes. Serve hot. You can make these up to six hours ahead. Let stand on baking sheets and reheat in 325- degree oven for five minutes just before serving. Makes about 26 biscuits

Recipe can be halved.

I have not written before, but I had to tell you that when we had a cool day this past week I made the scallion biscuits that I saw in your column. My husband is crazy about them. I am now being asked by our friends for the recipe which I am passing around. Thank you

*— **Janice and Bill***

Sweet Potato Minestrone with Turkey Sausage

A "make soup" class with Girl Scout leaders at camp

A comforting memory is soup simmering on the back of the stove on a cold day

This healthy recipe is low in fat, sodium, and sugar; no-one will know it though because it is seasoned well. This minestrone soup is loaded with "power veggies"; spinach, sweet potatoes, carrots, and tomatoes, making about six servings; I often double the recipe and freeze half.

INGREDIENTS: *½ pound smoked turkey sausage, cut into quarter-inch slices*

1 cup **each**; *chopped onion, chopped carrots*

¾ cup thinly sliced celery

2 to3 cups diced peeled sweet potatoes

1 teaspoon dried oregano

1 teaspoon cumin

½ to 1 teaspoon coarsely ground pepper, to taste.

3 cups water or broth

2 (14.5 ounce) cans no-salt-added whole tomatoes, undrained, coarsely chopped

1 (15 ounce) can great northern beans, rinsed and drained

8 cups coarsely chopped fresh spinach, washed well

Combine sausage, carrot, onion, and celery in a Dutch oven or soup pot over medium-high heat. Sauté for about 7 minutes or until sausage is browned. Add sweet potatoes, oregano, cumin, pepper, water, tomatoes, and beans; bring to a boil; cover, lower heat and simmer 30 to 45 minutes or until vegetables are tender.

Stir in spinach and cook an additional 10 minutes.

TIPS:
1. If you'd like the soup thickened, save out one-third of the beans; mash and add to soup.

2. Sausage can be browned first in the oven to remove fat.

3. Use more beans and omit sausage.

4. Use organic vegetables as often as you can, especially those without peels, such as peppers.

Comment from Diana T.   *I am making a second batch of sweet potato minestrone, it is that good.*

My First Macaroni and Cheese Bake Off

On January 15, 2011, New Hampshire Dairy Farmers hosted their first Macaroni & Cheese Bake Off at the Holiday Inn in Concord, New Hampshire. This was my first time entering one of my recipes, but this particular recipe has always been hugely popular.

I was pretty confident, but didn't know what to expect. Tickets were sold to the public for this event, and about three hundred people were expected, they would be the voters. Those who entered were asked to make two restaurant-sized pans for the taste testing; It turned out to be just enough. I knew I was in the running when several people came back for seconds.

The people at the next station were a grandmother with her granddaughter who entered Grandmothers' recipe, traditional elbow macaroni with a Velveeta cheese sauce. It was delicious, and reminded me of macaroni and cheese in the 1950's and "60's". I made sure to get that recipe.

One little girl about nine years old came back for thirds, and said to me that my macaroni and cheese was the only one she liked enough to finish and want more of. She came back again to tell me that she had just voted for my recipe. When the winners were being announced, she came to my station again to wait right next to me.

Talk about loyalty; I admired her conviction at such a young age.

I am very happy with my second place huge red ribbon. I left the hotel with a smile on my face, confident that this macaroni and cheese would be enjoyed by many people who took home the recipe today and will be enjoying it for years to come.

I first had this dish in the early 2000's at a bridal shower luncheon. I am not the only one who went home with the recipe that day. My friend and hostess said she had found the recipe in a magazine; it was that simple. That is the way it goes with a good recipe, passed from one cook to another for many, many years.

This macaroni and cheese will be around for a long time to come.

By the way, the recipe that took first place in the bake off was "Beefy Macaroni & Cheese" made with beef smoked sausage, three kinds of cheeses, and topped with French's onion rings. I never did get a chance to taste it, but I did take the recipe.

SECOND PLACE BAKED MACARONI & CHEESE

INGREDIENTS: *1 pound uncooked pasta (medium shells work well)*
3 cups shredded cheddar cheese
1 (10 3/4 ounce) can cream of mushroom soup
3/4 cup mayonnaise (if doubled use 1 cup)
2 (10 3/4 ounce) cans Campbell's cheddar cheese soup (if doubled use 3 cans)
1 cup buttery crackers, crushed, for topping

Cook pasta and drain. Combine cheese, soups, and mayonnaise; mix with cooked pasta. Place in a buttered 13"x 9" baking dish. Sprinkle with crushed crackers. Lightly drizzle with melted butter.

Bake covered at 350-degrees for 45 minutes. Uncover for another 15 minutes or till bubbly hot and lightly browned.

Tip: Children may not like the "black bits" (mushrooms) in the finished dish. To avoid this, use a mesh strainer to strain mushroom soup first.

RESPONSES TO MACARONI AND CHEESE

I just read the Tribune and was thrilled to see that you won second place in the bake off. My husband says that when you add sausage to macaroni and cheese, it is no longer macaroni and cheese, and that you probably should have taken first place. I am sure he is right. You should enter more contests like that!

— **Sharon**

Your macaroni and cheese was a hit. For my husband to say "Great job, Dear", is awesome. I finally found a recipe he likes. Now I would like to try the Beefy Mac & Cheese to see why it won first place. To be better than yours, it should jump off the plate into my mouth!

— *Thank you,* **Carol, Methuen MA**

*I'm in the process of adding your macaroni and cheese recipe to my collection, as it is one of my favorite foods. I would have **loved** to attend a Macaroni and Cheese Bake off!!*

— *Ann*

Friday I had guests and made your macaroni and cheese, everyone loved it. Thanks sooooo much. My hubby says "it's a keeper". In talking to friends, one woman said she did not like mushrooms and asked what could be substituted. Can you help us with that?

Thanks,
Priscilla

Note: There were times I did not use the mushroom soup and successfully substituted a béchamel sauce (butter, flour, milk, sprinkle of nutmeg). I made it about the same consistency as condensed soup, and the same amount, 10 ounces. It gave a nice, rich flavor.

Make a Big Batch of Marinara

Comments from Lorraine M.; *"Recently you had a spaghetti sauce in your article. I made it and everyone raved about it, better than my mother's recipe that takes 3 hours to make. Thank you and please continue writing your variety of great meals to make."*

Make this red sauce on Saturday and suppers for the coming week are a cinch.

Enjoy a spaghetti dinner on Sunday and on other evenings the choice is yours from baked ziti to delicious vegetable lasagna.

Marinara is truly a multipurpose sauce. It is perfect as is for many dishes, or by adding a few ingredients such as lemon rind or crushed red pepper you can hike it up a notch for shrimp or mussels recipes. Because you have already done most of the work by making the sauce, even a fancy dinner can be quick on a weeknight.

Making marinara is actually pretty quick; combine the ingredients, and let it simmer away to get the best flavor possible from the tomatoes and herbs. You are free to catch up on your errands, watch a good movie, play with the kids, and stir the pot every once-in-a-while.

To me there is nothing more inviting than coming into a house where a pot of "something good" is simmering away on the back of the stove; the aroma is what will greet you first.

Basic Marinara

3 tablespoons olive oil
3 cups chopped yellow onion (about 3 medium)
1 tablespoon sugar
3 tablespoons minced garlic (about 6 cloves)
2 teaspoons salt
2 teaspoons dried basil
1 ½ teaspoons dried oregano
1 teaspoon dried thyme
1 teaspoon fresh ground black pepper
½ teaspoon fennel seeds, crushed
2 tablespoons balsamic vinegar
2 cups fat-free, low-sodium chicken broth
3 (28 ounce) cans no- salt- added crushed tomatoes (I prefer Cento brand)

In a large stockpot heat oil over medium heat; Add onion and cook 4 minutes while stirring. Add sugar and next 7 ingredients (through fennel seeds); cook 1 minute stirring constantly. Stir in vinegar and cook 30 seconds. Add broth and tomatoes; bring to a simmer. Cook over low heat for at least an hour or until sauce thickens, stirring occasionally. (When cooking at a low simmer, just a few bubbles every few seconds will create the deepest taste.)

Note: Because marinara is simmered for a long time, dried herbs are best. They soften and maintain more flavor during a long cook time. Crumble them in your hand to release the essential oils.

Store sauce in refrigerator for up to 5 days or freeze for a few months. Makes about 12 cups.

THICKENING THE SAUCE

Stir occasionally so the top is pushed down into the pot, letting more of the liquid rise. As the tomatoes thicken, they also settle to the bottom and can scorch; stirring helps to prevent this.

The final sauce should be thick, but not as thick as tomato paste.

If the marinara seems too thick just add a little water, bringing back to a simmer and cooking a while longer.

MORE USES WITH MARINARA

1. Dipping sauce for crusty bread

2. Cover meatballs on a hoagie roll

3. On a hamburger with provolone cheese

4. Stir into green beans for a side dish.

If you haven't had stuffed shells lately, this would be a good way to use your freshly made sauce.

SPINACH AND RICOTTA-STUFFED SHELLS

Preheat oven to 350 degrees.
2 cups Basic Marinara sauce, divided
2 ½ cups ricotta cheese
½ cup parmesan cheese
½ teaspoon onion powder or dried onion
½ teaspoon dried basil
¼ teaspoon salt

¼ teaspoon pepper
1 (10 ounce) package frozen chopped spinach, thawed,
    drained and squeezed dry
1 large egg yolk
1 garlic clove, minced
24 cooked jumbo pasta shells

Spread ½ cup of sauce on the bottom of a 13x9 inch baking dish that has been lightly coated with cooking spray.

Combine ricotta, parmesan, onion powder, basil, salt, pepper, drained spinach, egg yolk, and garlic in a large bowl, stirring well.

Spoon about 1 ½ tablespoon filling into each pasta shell. Arrange stuffed shells in prepared dish; spread with remaining sauce, cover and bake for about 30 minutes. Let stand 5to10 minutes before serving.

While visiting my son in Telluride Colorado, I had the pleasure of meeting Honga, who is a fantastic cook and author of an exceptional cookbook that has a special place in my collection. Some of Honga's favorite recipes, and now mine, include Asian Pumpkin Soup, Coconut Curry mussels, Sweet & Sour Tofu, and Mango and Sticky Rice.

I love coconut and curry, but discovered there is so much more to Thai food. What I thought was too exotic and difficult for me to prepare, has now become quick and easy. I found an Asian market near home so that I can make most any dish.

Coconut Curry Chicken and Shrimp Soup

This Thai-influenced soup combines the spice of curry and the coolness of coconut milk for a pleasant balance. Use either more curry or more coconut milk to create the level of spice you desire.

You can also substitute beef, tofu, or fish for the chicken.

INGREDIENTS: *1 tablespoon high-temperature cooking oil (safflower, corn, peanut)*
1 small onion, diced
2 cloves garlic, minced
1 tablespoon Thai green curry paste
2 boneless chicken breasts cut into bite-size pieces
½ cup straw mushrooms
4 pea eggplants or 1 small Japanese eggplant, sliced (or small Italian eggplant)
14 ounces canned coconut milk
¼ cup chicken stock or water
1 inch of galangal, sliced
¼ stalk lemongrass, sliced

4 kaffir lime leaves
1 tablespoon fish sauce
1 tablespoon brown sugar
1 cup fresh shelled peas or shelled edamame, may use
  frozen, thawed
1 tablespoon fresh lemon juice
2 bok choy leaves, sliced
Fresh cilantro, chopped (garnish)

Preheat a wok or skillet over high heat until it just begins to smoke. Drizzle the oil down the sides of the wok and immediately add onion, garlic and curry paste, stirring occasionally. Add chicken and mushrooms. Stir for 1 minute.

Add eggplant, coconut milk and stock. Stir quickly, then add galangal, lemongrass, lime leaves, fish sauce, brown sugar and peas. Stir again; making sure curry paste is blended throughout the dish. Let simmer for 2 minutes.

When chicken is cooked through, stir in lemon juice and turn off the heat.

Add bok choy and stir, allowing the remaining heat to cook the bok choy; Makes 2 servings.

Top with cilantro and serve with rice.

COMMON INGREDIENTS IN THAI COOKING:

Kaffir: Many Thai recipes call for kaffir lime leaves. If the leaf is used whole, like in curry or in soup, most people do not eat the leaf itself. Substitute 1 tablespoon lime zest for 6 kaffir leaves.

Lemongrass: A common ingredient in Thai cooking, lemongrass provides a zesty lemon flavor and aroma to many Thai dishes. Lemon juice may be substituted for lemongrass in a pinch.

Galangal: Fresh minced ginger root can work as an alternative to its more exotic counterpart. Use about one and a half times as much ginger as the recipe calls for in galangal. This will ensure that your recipe is sufficiently potent.

Straw mushrooms are as common in Thailand as white button mushrooms are in the US. Straw mushrooms are meaty and mild in flavor. Canned straw mushrooms are available at most Asian markets. Generally, the straw mushrooms themselves are not the driving flavor; you can substitute using porcini mushrooms.

Most of these ingredients can be found in an Asian market and some can be found in our local supermarkets, as in baby purple eggplants which are in most markets today and several kinds of exotic mushrooms are now commonly found.

RHUBARB; TIPS & GROWING

Our family rhubarb recipes go back at least five generations according to my grandfather. My mother made the most delicious rhubarb-strawberry jam, and always a batch of sugar free for the diet conscience. My grandmother was famous for her rhubarb pies, and my Aunt made the most incredible rhubarb-almond cobbler. If you are not familiar with rhubarb, as many people are not, try some rhubarb recipes. You may be pleasantly surprised and understand why this has been a staple in New England gardens, and enjoyed in New England homes for generations. These days, you can easily find it in the produce section of your supermarket.

When purchasing rhubarb choose firm stalks that are deep in color. They will stay fresh in sealed plastic bags in refrigerator up to one week. One pound of rhubarb yields approximately four cups of cut-up rhubarb.

Tips I have received from friends & readers:

1. Use homemade strawberry-rhubarb sauce on oatmeal and pancakes.

2. Freeze rhubarb in plastic freezer bags; two and one-half cups in each bag.

   Also, blanching rhubarb in boiling water for one minute and cooling promptly in ice water helps to retain color and flavor when freezing.

3. I make rhubarb jam which I give for gifts. It makes a great dipping sauce for pretzels, and when warmed is delicious on ice cream.

CARAMEL RHUBARB COBBLER

This is an old fashioned dessert with a biscuit like topping.

INGREDIENTS: *7 tablespoons butter or margarine, divided*
3/4 cup packed brown sugar
1/2 cup sugar, divided
3 tablespoons cornstarch
1 ¼ cups water
6 cups chopped fresh or frozen rhubarb, thawed
1 ¼ cups all purpose flour

1 ½ teaspoons baking powder
¼ teaspoon salt
1/3 cup milk
Cinnamon-sugar
Vanilla ice cream or whipped cream (optional)

In saucepan over medium heat, melt three tablespoons butter. Add brown sugar, ¼ cup of the sugar and the cornstarch. Gradually stir in water and rhubarb; cook and stir until thickened, about 5-8 minutes.

Pour into a greased 2-quart baking dish and set aside.

Topping: In a bowl, combine flour, baking powder, salt and remaining ¼ cup sugar. Melt remaining butter; add to dry ingredients with milk. Mix well. Drop by a tablespoon-full onto rhubarb mixture.

Bake at 350 degrees for 35-40 minutes until fruit is bubbly and the top golden brown. Sprinkle with cinnamon-sugar. Serve warm with vanilla ice cream or whipped cream if desired. Makes 5-6 servings.

GROW YOUR OWN

For those of you who would like to grow your own; purchase plants, put in a sunny spot, and you will enjoy it for many years. Rhubarb plants can be transplanted successfully. My father transplanted his six rhubarb plants to Cape Cod when they retired there, and those plants lasted another thirteen years.

1. Plant rhubarb roots two to three feet apart in rich, well-drained soil, worked to a depth of a foot or more.
   You can add compost, peat moss or other organic material, plus lime and fertilizer before planting.

2. Pull any weeds in the spring before the rhubarb starts to grow. Waiting until later could damage the roots, causing decay or disease.

3. Don't pick rhubarb the year you plant it. Instead, pick lightly the second season. Do not remove more than two-thirds of the stalks at a time.

RHUBARB CUSTARD BARS

Once I tried these delicious bars, the recipe went into my favorites, and became a winner with family and friends. I bake these at least once during rhubarb season.

Preheat oven to 350 degrees

INGREDIENTS: *2 cups all-purpose flour*
¼ cup sugar
1 cup cold butter
FILLING: *2 cups sugar*
7 tablespoons flour
1 cup whipping cream
3 eggs, beaten
5 cups finely chopped fresh or frozen rhubarb. If frozen, thaw and drain **well.**
TOPPING: *2 packages (3 ounces each) cream cheese, softened*
½ cup sugar
½ teaspoon vanilla extract
1 cup whipping cream, whipped

In a bowl, combine flour and sugar; cut in butter until mixture resembles coarse crumbs. Press into a greased 13x9x2 inch baking pan. Bake at 350 degrees for 10 minutes. Meanwhile make filling; combine sugar and flour in a bowl. Whisk in cream and eggs. Stir in rhubarb. Pour over hot crust. Bake at 350 degrees for 40- 45 minutes, or until custard is set; cool.

For topping, beat cream cheese, sugar and vanilla till smooth; fold in whipped cream. Spread over cooled bars, cover and chill. Cut into bars. Keep refrigerated till 1 hour before serving (at room temperature).

Makes approximately 3 dozen bars.

COMMENTS FROM RHUBARB FANS:

"We are fans of rhubarb, and I make a pie similar to your 'sissy pie". An old friend gave me the recipe saying the secret to the pie is in the eggs. He was an experienced baker working in pastry shops years ago.

— Thank you" **N.L.L.**

"Thank you for sending the packet of rhubarb recipes. I shared them with fellow gardeners at our annual plant sale and they were very excited about some new rhubarb recipes, and such a variety. The caramel rhubarb cobbler is delicious and a favorite."

*— **Grace M. Windham NH***

"My parents live in WA and grow a ton of rhubarb, so we are looking forward to trying your rhubarb-custard pie, bars, and the cobbler".

*— **Rowan***

"My mother-in-law lives in Indiana, makes great rhubarb-strawberry jam and rhubarb desserts. I mailed her your column with the "sissy pie" recipe

and she was thrilled. She'd love the cobbler recipe, if you could e-mail it to me. I look forward to reading your column every week, and have made many of your recipes."

*— **Rosemary B, Methuen***

"It surprises friends of mine that rhubarb is so popular in New England, pleasantly so as they love everything I have made with our rhubarb. I enjoyed reading how your family has grown it for generations, and thanks for the new recipes."

*— **Carol, Salem***

"A note to thank you for some great recipes; the Easy Rhubarb Dessert was so delightful my husband asked me to make it again, and boy, does that make me feel good. Love your column,

*— **Bess, Windham***

"My Aunt has lots of rhubarb growing in her yard, please send me any recipes you have for rhubarb, she is looking forward to some new ways to use it."

*— **Diane T, Methuen***

"My family is very fond of rhubarb pies and cobblers. I would greatly appreciate you sending me the caramel-rhubarb recipe mentioned in your column so I can start cooking."

*— **Don B.***

(See Chapters 1 and 4 for more rhubarb recipes.)

Apples and an Orchard Wedding

The sun was shining on a September day when I attended a beautiful wedding in an apple orchard in the town of Easthampton, a lovely small college town in the western part of Massachusetts, where rolling fields, country Inns, and miles of farmland welcome you.

I arrived at Park Hill Orchard to find the ceremony being held on a gently sloping hill overlooking the orchards. This is where friends and family were seated waiting to see Tatyana and Joe become husband and wife.

I have known Joe since he was in the third grade and became friends with my son and came to a Halloween party I gave for the kids. That was the beginning of Joe regularly being in my home, and here I am, years later, watching him marry the woman he loves. From the first time I was with Joe and Tatyana I felt that they brought out the best in each other. Tatyana is beautiful inside and out and still carries her lovely Russian accent so nicely that I could listen to her speak forever.

Joe and Tatyana tell how they met:

"Tatyana and I met at a bar nicknamed "the beer can museum" for its collection of 4000+ beer cans. We were both out of our element. I stopped going to bars years ago and so did Tatyana. She was with friends celebrating her best friend's promotion, and I was with my brother who was visiting. But there we were on bar stools side by side.

Tatyana decided to see what my story was. I immediately shrugged her off as I was enjoying my brother's company and was quick to pass judgment. But I found myself taking a few looks and listening in a bit. My brother had a better view though, and was totally egging me on. I remember when our eyes caught, and I think it was over at that moment! We were quick to move to the juke box together. Eventually I passed her my phone number. It was a few days before that call came, but the rest is history…" J & T

I glance at Joe as his bride walks to him on the arm of her father. She is "bride beautiful" in a satin gown that shines in the sun.

They say their vows to each other as they stand on a platform built by Joe and his father-in-law, designed so that it will eventually become a part of the deck at their future home.

After the ceremony, guests make their way down a small hill guided by a roped-off path, with framed quotations about love and marriage along the way, soon coming to the huge white tent in the midst of the apple trees.

Here is where about 120 people with much happiness and revelry welcomed just married Mr. and Mrs. Joseph Delaney to the party. And a wonderful party it was; fun music to dance a conga, watching the bride and groom enjoying their first dance as husband and wife, eating a spectacular meal, and simply having a great time.

The cake was a beautiful confection of spice and apples with cream cheese frosting between the seven layers; and I have never had a wedding cake that was so moist, and as delicious to eat as it was beautiful.

I learned a bit of apple history that is relevant to Tatyana in particular. Remember I mentioned that she is Russian. There is a remote area in Russia called Alma Ata, which means "father of the apple", nearly two hundred miles from the capital city of Kazakhstan, the area Tatyana is from. Botanists believe this is where the first apple trees took root, the apple's Garden of Eden. According to a story written in the National Geographic, botanists travel to this area to collect seeds (genetic material) from the thousands of apple trees that grow wild here. The seeds are stored in freezers that serve as a gene bank for apples, and then planted in an orchard in Geneva NY to produce more apples for us to choose from and enjoy, as we certainly are on this day surrounded by an apple orchard.

Back at the reception, guests do not leave without stopping at a large pushcart with five huge bins that contained shiny apples; Macintosh, striped graven stein, ruby Mac's, Cortland, and Paula red's, and filling a bag to take home and enjoy.

THE WEDDING CAKE; APPLE SPICE CAKE
Recipe Courtesy of Margarita Dzyubenko, Event Planner and Baker

Thank you to Margarita for converting the wedding cake ingredients into a choice of three sizes that can be easily made at home.

INGREDIENTS: *2 cups all purpose flour*
2 teaspoons baking soda
2 teaspoons baking powder
½ teaspoon salt
3 teaspoons ground cinnamon
4 eggs
1 ¼ cups oil
1 cup granulated white sugar
1 cup packed brown sugar
2 teaspoons vanilla
3 small apples, peeled and grated
1 cup nuts (pecans or walnuts) optional
1 cup raisins - optional
Cream Cheese Frosting:
8 ounces cream cheese, softened
1/2 cup butter, softened
2 cups confectioners' sugar

1 teaspoon vanilla extract

Preheat oven to 325° (Baking slow keeps cake moist)

Prepare **two 9" pans, one 12" cake pan, or one 9"x 13"** pan by lining with parchment paper.

Mix together in a bowl, flour, baking soda, baking powder, salt, and cinnamon.

In a larger bowl, whisk together eggs, oil, sugars, and vanilla for a minute or so.

Add dry ingredients to the wet mixture, mix for 2 minutes. Add grated apples. Add nuts and raisins if desired. Pour batter into prepared cake pans and bake for approximately 40 - 50 minutes. Test for doneness by inserting a skewer, it should be dry when taken out. Cool then fill and frost with cream cheese frosting. Garnish with nuts.

PASTRY; CINNAMON ROLL-UPS
"JUST A MINUTES"

One of my favorite food memories growing up was my mother making pies. She was a champion pie baker, as were my grandmother and great grandmother; but what I absolutely loved was the magic made with the leftover pie dough. As my grandmother did before her, Mom rolled out scraps of dough and spread on a thin coating of butter, actually margarine. Next, she would sprinkle cinnamon sugar on, roll up into a log shape and cut them a good inch to 1 ¼ inch. When asked for the recipe, I named them "Cinnamon Roll-Ups", but in our family and with close friends, they are known as "just a minutes", deriving that name many years ago when eight children, father, grandfather, and uncles, would smell those baking and consistently ask "are they ready", "aren't they ready yet", and my mother's answer was always.....you got it, "in just a minute". To this day, many of us are just as happy to forego a pie, if we can get plenty of "just a minutes". When it comes to food memories, you can never forget the smell of pastry dough and cinnamon baking in the oven.

When you bake pies, make extra dough and try these cinnamon roll-ups. Whoever is in the house will find their way to the kitchen very quickly, and you might find yourself creating a new family tradition, and a delectable food memory.

This is my mother's favorite pie crust recipe. She used it consistently, whether for savory or sweet pies. It always came out flaky, tasty, and holds up to handling.

When making pastry ahead, wrap tightly in plastic and refrigerate for few days or frozen for several weeks.

STELLA JACKMAN'S PASTRY RECIPE; DOUBLE-CRUST PIE:

MIX TOGETHER: *2 cups all purpose flour*
1 teaspoon salt
2 teaspoons sugar
Cut in 3/4 cup cold solid shortening until crumbly
*   using a pastry blender or 2 knives.*
Mix together:
1/3 cup cold water
2 teaspoons white vinegar
1 large egg

Shake or whisk well;

Add to flour/shortening mixture, mixing together with a large fork till it forms a ball.

MAKE CINNAMON ROLL-UPS

Roll out dough into a rectangle shape until dough is fairly thin without tearing.

Using approximately ¾ stick of very soft butter, spread with your fingers to lightly cover dough, right to the edges (use only enough butter to lightly cover the dough). Sprinkle with cinnamon-sugar until dough is covered.

Starting with long side closest to you, roll up dough keeping it as tight as you can (the first couple of inches will test your patience, but then it goes smoothly). When at the end, use your fingers to moisten the edges lightly with water so it will stick to the roll.

Use a pastry cutter or non-serrated sharp knife to cut the pastry into 1 inch pieces.

Place roll-ups an inch apart on a cookie sheet lined with parchment paper.

Bake at 375 degrees for 25-30 minutes, until pastry is a light golden brown.

PASTRY TIPS:

Liquid: Most recipes call for water to allow flour to form gluten and let the dough stick together. Add too little liquid, and you'll have trouble molding a crust, but overdo it, and your pie bottom will be too hard.

Vinegar can serve two useful roles in pie crusts; it promotes tenderness and can keep crust from getting too brown. The acidity of vinegar reduces gluten in the dough, making it flaky and tender. The dough will also roll out more easily, shrink less during baking, and in essence be more forgiving and patchable.

Any pie crust recipe can be easily modified by substituting 1 tablespoon of the water with white or cider vinegar.

Fat: Fat lends flavor, especially if you're using butter. Plus, it gives the dough flakiness because chunks of butter coat the flour. This is why you don't want to cut butter too small or have it at room temperature. When making pie crust, many bakers use half butter and half solid shortening such as Crisco.

Salt: Even in desserts a pinch of salt peaks the flavor.

A Special Letter; Children and Leftover Pie Dough

I received a letter that I would like to tell you about; it refers to "Cinnamon Roll-Ups", using leftover pie dough, and children.

Alyce is retired now, but when reading about my use of leftover pie dough, it brought back memories of her many years of caring for children in her home, often with children that had been abused and neglected and were referred by agencies. She stated that two to three times a week she would bake with the children, which she said they responded to, and loved doing, often making pie crust so they could make cinnamon pin-wheels or sticks. Each child was provided with their own bowl and rolling pin. "To see the look on their faces", Alyce explains, "was my reward"; pensive when rolling dough, happy when playing with flour, ecstatic when seeing a tray of baked cinnamon sticks come out of the oven.

I'm sure Alyce didn't think of the therapy of this activity, but I can see how children would benefit from working with their hands and molding dough, the feelings of accomplishment and approval, and just plain enjoyment. My guess is when they left Alyce's kitchen it was with more than flour on their faces and baked goodies.

I send special accolades to Alyce for all her years of work with the children, and to all those that work in or with Child-Care Agencies; your efforts are appreciated.

— Sincerely, Pat

I Got It! THE Famous Jordan Marsh Blueberry Muffins

The first floor of the flagship store Jordan Marsh had a bakery famous for its blueberry muffins. Since the bakery closed in the early 1990s, the blueberry muffins have become the focus of much lore around the Boston area. A December 2004 Boston Globe newspaper article said, "For decades, any decent downtown shopping trip ended at Jordan Marsh, where the promise of a sugar-crusted blueberry muffin could make annoying children angelic."

The shopping mall, Shoppers World, opened in Framingham, Massachusetts on October 4, 1951 with Jordan Marsh at the southern end, unmistakable for its large white dome, and also developing a bakery that became popular for excellent quality bakery products. It was the blueberry muffins though that everyone raved about, and for many years the recipe was kept secret.

I grew up about thirty minutes from Framingham and would often shop at Shopper's World.

One day I decided to stop at the bakery, not thinking about the blueberry muffin recipe. I was waiting for my purchases to be bagged when an employee came out with a big tray of blueberry muffins to slide into the glass display case. I was right in front of him and just struck up a conversation about the recipe and how I would love to have it as my mother was such a good baker. He asked me if I had a pen and paper and he verbally told me the recipe as I frantically wrote it down. All I had in my purse was a pen that wrote in red ink and a card from the hospital where I worked and I wrote on the back of that. I used that recipe often before I noticed the vanilla extract missing. I made a batch adding 1 teaspoon vanilla, and a batch without. There was a very slight taste difference but I truly thought the blueberry flavor was more pronounced in the batch without the vanilla, so I continue to make them without vanilla.

That was 1971 and I have kept that card all this time.

JORDAN MARSH BLUEBERRY MUFFINS

Makes 1 dozen

Preheat oven to 375 degrees.

Grease and lightly flour muffin tins.

INGREDIENTS: *1/2 cup butter plus 2 tablespoons (do not substitute)*
1 and 1/4 cups sugar
2 eggs
1/2 cup whole milk
2 cups all-purpose flour (I prefer King Arthur brand)

> *2 teaspoons baking powder*
> *1/2 teaspoon salt*
> *2 ½ cups blueberries (in recent years I increased the*
> *amount of blueberries to 3 cups and floured them*
> *before adding to the batter)*
> *2 teaspoons sugar for topping*

Cream butter and sugar well, until light and fluffy; Add eggs one at a time, mixing well after each. Sift dry ingredients and alternate with milk into creamed mixture.

Mash ½ cup of the berries and stir in by hand. (Use a liberal amount of berries and mash very well. This really flavors the entire batter)

Toss the remaining blueberries with just a little flour to lightly coat, than add whole and stir by hand gently till mixed in.

Pile high in prepared muffin tins. Sprinkle sugar on top. Bake for 25 to 30 minutes.

Cool 30 minutes before removing from tins.

Note: There are several variations of Jordan Marsh blueberry muffins on the internet.

Hi Pat, Is it too late for you to send me the Jordan Marsh Blueberry muffin recipe? Your mentioning it brought back a memory of my mother driving to the Jordan Marsh in Peabody, and always bringing back those muffins. Thank you for bringing back a nice memory.

— **Cara, Haverhill**

Comment from Diane   *I remember those muffins and the story, now I too have the recipe and I thank you.*

Comments from Cara, Haverhill   *I'm so happy to see the Jordan Marsh blueberry muffin recipe, it brought back a memory of my mother driving to Jordan Marsh in Peabody and always bringing back those delicious muffins; thank you for sparking a nice memory.*

Comment from Helena   *I can't wait to show my Texas friends how muffins are supposed to be. Thank you for the Jordan Marsh blueberry muffin recipe and other recipes I have really liked.*

Comment from Eleanor, Salem NH   *I was thrilled to see the JM Blueberry muffin recipe in your article. They were one of the highlights, and now a good memory, of my trips to Jordan Marsh.*

CHAPTER 2
FAMILY

Family stories such as picking blueberries high on a hill, and how we coped with the resulting 24 quarts; and are you really a sissy if you eat this pie, with a wink and a grin, my grandfather said yes; and do you know the difference between a full-corn moon or Harvest moon and why that was important on a farm at harvest time; tid-bits of information within these stories about life, camaraderie and memories that make up a recipe collection.

Most recipes in this chapter are ones requested at family reunion's; made for years or generations by a grandmother or Aunt, and often come served in an antique dish that was once on *their* table…Memories with love!

Enjoy reading of our last Family Reunion held in the White Mountains of New Hampshire, with many ideas and tips that made our Reunion run smoothly.

RHUBARB CUSTARD PIE (SISSY PIE)
PEACHES & CREAM CHEESE-CAKE-PIE
BLUEBERRY CREAM PIE
BLUEBERRY SHORTCAKE OUR WAY
PINEAPPLE ZUCCHINI BREAD
QUICK STIR FRY ZUCCHINI
LOW COUNTRY SHRIMP BOIL
BAKED YELLOW EYE BEANS WITH PORK CHOPS
SPICY CLAMS WITH PORTUGUESE CHOURICO
SHORTCUT FOCCACIA
COUNTRY STYLE CORN PUDDING

Lime Sherbet Punch
MikeT's Sweet-White Potato Salad
Martha's Baked Stuffed Tomatoes
Family

Whereas Gourmet recipes of today take superb talent, and 'showcase" food beautifully, Family recipes have history; a memory often triggered simply by the aroma of something cooking. Often made for many years by family members and close friends, these are the recipes of tradition, and in my case, a collection of recipes from the strong women of my past that represent many years cooking for their families and for enjoyment. This was their time; raising their children, working with and caring for husbands, spoiling and loving grandchildren. Many of these recipes are handwritten, stained from use, with lovely personal notes written in margins; definitely not just a recipe, but a representation of the love, camaraderie, and memories that makes up a woman's recipe collection.

Real Men Do Eat this Pie!

The first person I am aware of that made this pie was my great-grand-mother Dagenais; she called it rhubarb-egg, by simply dropping three beaten eggs over sugared rhubarb. Her family loved the flavor combination, and from then on when she made plain rhubarb pies, she would also make rhubarb-egg. My grandmother followed this course, as did my mother, and somewhere along the way additions were made to create the version we now enjoy and call rhubarb-custard.

It was nearly fifty years ago that my father, his brother Leon, and their father, were having lunch at the kitchen table, my mother having just made several rhubarb pies including rhubarb-custard, her favorite. Two of my young brothers joined Mom in going for seconds on the rhubarb-custard, the men started to tease that "real men" eat plain rhubarb, and not "sissy pie" with custard. It was an affectionate tease that remains today, hence the name "sissy pie" has stuck.

My family fully loves anything with rhubarb, and we look forward to April to June when we can pick it fresh as my father and grandfather did on their farms all their lives.

RHUBARB-CUSTARD PIE (LOVINGLY CALLED "SISSY PIE")

INGREDIENTS: *9 inch pastry crust; bought pre-made or Stella Jackman's No Fail pie crust recipe: (See Chapter 1 for recipe)*
5 ½ cups rhubarb, cut in half-inch pieces
1 and 1/2 cups sugar
3 large eggs
1 tablespoons whole milk
3 tablespoons flour
1/4 cup additional sugar
1 teaspoon vanilla
¼ teaspoon salt (or as my grandmother would say "couple of pinches")

Combine rhubarb with 1 ½ cup sugar. Put into pie plate lined with bottom crust. Beat together remaining ingredients until flour is dissolved. Pour over the rhubarb. Bake at 400 degrees for 15 minutes, than 350 degrees for 40 to 50 minutes or till set and rhubarb soft. Top crust not necessary, but at times I top uncooked pie with decorative pastry shapes or strips.

Peaches & Cream Cheese-Cake-Pie

Always searching for the next family favorite, my mother found it in this recipe. After making a few times she knew it was "a keeper". We found it hard to define exactly what it was; it's a bit of cheese-cake, a fruit layer like pie, and a little bit cake. My young nephew, Justin, solved the issue one day when he said "Grammy, could you make the cheese-cake-pie?" Children do simplify things!

We all came to have a favorite flavor; blueberry, peach, and apple were the versions she made frequently. The fresh peach started it all which remains my favorite.

INGREDIENTS: *¾ cup all-purpose flour*
1 teaspoon baking powder
½ teaspoon salt
1 egg
3 tablespoons soft butter
½ cup milk
*1 small package vanilla pudding mix (**not** instant)*
6 to 8 fresh peaches, very ripe
1(8 ounce) package cream cheese, softened
3 tablespoons apple juice
½ cup sugar
1 tablespoon sugar mixed with ½ teaspoon cinnamon

Combine flour, baking powder, salt, egg, butter, milk, and pudding mix in a small bowl, beat for two minutes. Pour into a large greased pie plate or 9 inch cake pan. Arrange sliced fruit over the batter. In a small bowl, combine cream cheese, apple juice and ½ cup sugar. Beat 2 minutes, than spoon on top of fruit coming to within 1 inch of edge. Sprinkle with cinnamon/sugar mixture. Bake at 350 degrees for 35 to 40 minutes. (If using apples sauté in butter to slightly soften).

High on a Hill Picking Sweet Blueberries

My father was raised to not waste food, and when you have eight children you take that seriously. Blueberries are food, and even if they are wild and on bushes high on a hill, you pick them. My father had to make this a worthwhile full-day excursion which meant as many people as he could get to help him pick. His father and brother Leon would often go, along with three or four kids in tow. It was tedious work and this one particular day the hill was prolific with ripe blueberries and they picked and picked until it was too dark to see. He ended up using a flashlight from the car for a while. When they finally arrived home exhaustion was apparent (as was my mother's wrath), but quickly the children were fed and flopped into bed. It was now my mother and I who needed to pick over the berries and get them into freezer boxes as they would get mushy sitting overnight. It took hours to remove the twigs and leaves that come with fresh picked blueberries, but as a family we had picked and frozen 24 quarts. My mother and father got great joy just looking into that upright full freezer. We had enough berries for the year ahead for all our favorites; muffins, pie, and most of all, blueberry shortcake with homemade biscuits.

Blueberry Cream Pie, Recipe courtesy April's Mom

Note the use of "Dream Whip" which was very popular in the 1950's and '60's

Mix together (1) 8 ounce package cream cheese, 1 cup sugar and 2 envelopes Dream Whip (can be found in baking aisle). Slice 2 bananas and place on bottom of a pre-made pie crust (good with graham cracker or pastry crust); sprinkle with lemon juice; Spoon cream mixture on top of bananas. Mix 1 cup fresh blueberries with 1 can blueberry pie filling; spread on top of cream filling. Refrigerate 4 hours.

There is no written recipe for our **Blueberry Shortcake**, but it is very simple; lightly mash (use potato masher) freshly washed blueberries, add sugar until sweetened to your taste and let sit until well dissolved. Bake up some baking powder biscuits; cut one in half, top with blueberries, then top with softened vanilla ice cream OR fresh whipped cream.

My favorite is with ice cream melting all over the blueberries. Enjoy!

Pineapple Zucchini Bread

Within my mother's recipe collection were five different recipes for zucchini bread. The following was her favorite; the only recipe with crushed pineapple in it. Moist and delicious, she loved that it was given to her by a good friend, Aggie Kinnas. Aggie and Mom shared their love of baking more than cooking, and that contributed to a long friendship, and sharing recipes.

Makes 2 loaves

INGREDIENTS: *2 large eggs*
1and 1/3 cups sugar
1 cup vegetable oil
2 teaspoons vanilla extract
2 cups shredded zucchini, unpeeled (remove large seeds)
1 (8 ounce) can crushed pineapple, drained
1 ½ cups all-purpose flour
1 ½ cups whole wheat flour

2 teaspoons baking soda
½ teaspoon baking powder
1 teaspoon salt
1 ½ teaspoons cinnamon
¾ teaspoon nutmeg
1 cup chopped pecans or walnuts
1 cup raisins or currants

Beat eggs at medium speed with electric mixer until foamy. Add sugar, oil, and vanilla; beat 2 minutes or until mixture is slightly thickened. Stir in zucchini and pineapple. Combine flours and spices; add to zucchini mixture, stirring just until blended. Stir in pecans and raisins. Pour into 2 greased and floured 8 ½ x 4 ½ x 3 inch loaf pans. Bake at 350 degrees 50-55 minutes or when toothpick inserted in center comes out clean. Cool in pans 10 minutes, and then remove from pans to cool completely on a wire rack.

Quick Stir Fry Zucchini: Who'd ever think something so simple could taste so good?

Wash 2 medium zucchini, slice into ¼ inch rounds. Heat 3-4 table-spoons sesame oil until it just begins to smoke. Add zucchini, stir, and sauté till tender. Remove from pan with a slotted spoon, sprinkle with toasted sesame seeds.

Tips: 1. Use your zucchini up by slicing it in three to four- cup batches, and put in freezer bags to use during the winter; when ready to use thaw in paper-towel lined strainer.

2. If you want to freeze for a later batch of zucchini bread, shred in processor or blender (unpeeled), drain in paper-towel lined strainer for 2-3 hours, than put in freezer bags in 2-cup batches, dating and marking clearly.

Driving Thru Maryland's Eastern Shore

My husband and I were traveling through the Eastern Shore area of Maryland returning home from ten days touring Virginia. We were looking for a place for supper. Curious about signs for "Low Country Boil', which we hadn't heard of in New England, we chose a rustic place to stop and check it out.

We ordered the low country shrimp boil for two. We sat on their deck at a picnic table, with charming lanterns and red-checked plastic table-cloths. The waitress covered the tablecloth with brown paper, and then came out carrying a huge pot which she poured out onto the table; a steaming-hot one-pot dish loaded with shrimp, crab, corn on the cob, smoked sausage and small potatoes and onions. We had dishes, napkins, and forks, but watching others around us, most people were eating with their fingers. It was definitely casual, and wonderfully festive.

Since that time I have made this at home for get-togethers in my back-yard, the best meal for a warm evening in August. There are endless varieties of "Low Country Boils" (that originated in the low country of South Carolina) and here is the way I like to make it.

Low Country Shrimp Boil

INGREDIENTS: *2 lemons, halved, plus more for serving*
3 bay leaves
2 teaspoons salt
¼ cup Old bay seasoning

4 medium onions, halved
1 head garlic, halved
3 pounds red potatoes, medium to large size
4 ears corn, husked and broken in half
2 pounds smoked sausage, such as kielbasa (cut into 4 inch pieces)
Extra large shrimp, 5 to 7 per person depending on size
½ stick butter
Hot pepper sauce and Cocktail sauce for condiments

Fill a huge pot with four to five quarts of water. (The water level will rise as you fill it with the solid ingredients, so be careful not to fill more than half-way). Squeeze lemon juice into the water, tossing in the halves too. Add bay leaves, salt, seasoning, and garlic. Bring broth to a boil and simmer for twenty minutes. You want a very aromatic broth with plenty of salt and spices, so taste it. Don't be afraid to make it strong so that the flavor penetrates the sausage and vegetables. If your potatoes are large, halve them. Add to pot with the onions and sausage, simmer for 10 minutes. Now add corn and cook another 10 minutes, making sure everything stays covered in liquid. Toss in the shrimp, shut off the heat, and cover the pot; Let sit for 15 minutes. **Drain liquid off**, add butter and salt and pepper to taste. Have your guests seated and serve in a wide low bowl or by piling onto the center of the table. (This is where plastic disposable tablecloths come in handy). Have lemons and plenty of napkins available. Serves 6-8

CAPE COD FISHERMAN MAKES A GREAT POT OF BAKED BEANS.

A son remembers: "My father, George Earl Jackman Jr., was an avid outdoorsman. Whether it was fly-fishing the rivers and lakes of New Hampshire and Maine, hunting deer in New Hampshire, or hand lining for cod and haddock from our boat on Cape Cod, he spent as much time outdoors as he could. If he wasn't fishing or hunting, he'd be working in the garden, or out in the bay, scalloping or clamming. I'd go out fishing with Dad fairly often, even though I'd be hanging my head over the side of the boat as much as I'd fish.

It was a tough day, getting up around three a.m. to be out on the fishing grounds by six a.m., and back to the Chatham Fish Pier close to five p.m., and Dad would do it six days a week.

We kept our strength up by eating cold bean sandwiches with mayonnaise and a slice of onion on them for lunch, still one of my favorite lunches to this day.

I'm not sure how many variations Dad and Mom tried before coming up with this final baked bean recipe, but I'm glad they put in the effort. I can't remember anyone who's tried them that didn't ask for more, and the recipe.

I use a Crockpot to cut down on electric usage and heat, rather than the oven, and can't tell the difference."

— *Bud Jackman*

YELLOW EYE BAKED BEANS; RECIPE
COURTESY OF BUD JACKMAN

INGREDIENTS: *4-6 medium size pork chops*
1 pound dried yellow eye beans, picked over
¼ pound salt pork cut in 2 inch pieces
2/3 cup sugar
2 tablespoons dry mustard
2 teaspoons salt

¼ teaspoon black pepper
2 medium whole onions, optional

Soak beans in cold water to cover for several hours. Then bring to a boil, turn off heat, cover and let sit overnight.

Next morning, drain beans, saving liquid. Put salt pork and all seasoning in baking pan, add beans, and cover with saved liquid adding water if needed to just cover beans. Brown pork chops in a skillet and place on beans.

Bake uncovered 6 to 8 hours at 275 degrees. Add water when beans become dry.

MY FAMILY AND I CHERISH OUR MEMORIES OF CAPE COD;

My Grandmother, Mary Oles, started it all in 1930 when she answered a help wanted ad for a housekeeper. She travelled from Oxford, Massachusetts to East Harwich to meet Mr. Edgar Wilbur, the gentleman advertising for help. The rest is history as the little cottage on Pleasant Bay Road became her home until her death in 1978.

Cooking and baking were not Nana Oles's best talents, but she made fantastic Pierogi's, never using a written recipe, but filling her kitchen with flour and dough as she made bowls of them for her company and family, topped with butter and a large dollop of sour cream.

Another constant on her kitchen counter was a gallon jar of pickled eggs that she kept filled, telling me that if you want to enjoy a "jigger" of vodka, you must have it with an egg, which she further explained is the Polish way; works for me!

Nana and Ned's small cottage on Pleasant Bay Road became our family vacation spot from 1942 to 2002. Most all of the "Oles" families vacationed there many summers during those years, enjoying Harding's beach in Chatham, the movie theater on main street on a rainy day, the Chatham lighthouse, leisurely walks to Pleasant Bay, sleeping in an old chicken coop and using an outhouse (not a good memory) and eating a lot of clams and quahogs, which Ned and his "cronies" dug from the shore at North Beach. I remember sitting on the grass in a circle while Dad and Ned shucked (opened) the clams, and we took turns eating them raw, which I never got enough of.

SPICY CLAMS WITH PORTUGUESE CHOURICO

INGREDIENTS: *4 pounds steamer clams*
1 tablespoon olive oil
8 ounces chorizo, halved lengthwise and thinly sliced (if you can't find chourico, substitute with the Spanish sausage chorizo, which is similar).
1 tablespoon minced garlic
2 teaspoons paprika
¼ teaspoon fresh ground black pepper
1 teaspoon crushed red pepper flakes
1 large onion, thinly sliced
1 (14.5 ounce) can diced tomatoes, well drained
½ cup dry white wine such as Pinot Grigio
1/3 cup finely chopped cilantro or parsley

Scrub clams if they are muddy or sandy. Rinse in sink or large bowl of cold water, drain well; Repeat, allowing clams to sit in water until time to cook them.

In large covered pot, heat oil over medium-high heat. When hot, add sausage, garlic, paprika, pepper and pepper flakes, and onion. Cook and stir until onion begins to soften, 4-5 minutes.

Add tomatoes and wine. Simmer for 10 minutes. Stir in cilantro or parsley and transfer half the sauce to a bowl or large measuring cup. Lift clams out of water and add them to the pot. Pour sauce from bowl onto clams and cover. Cook for 10 to 12 minutes, or until clams open. Discard any clams that do not open during cooking. Pour clams and sauce into a large serving bowl, or divide into 6 individual serving bowls. Serve with crusty bread to sop up the broth, a light wine, and invite friends!

As an accompaniment to any pasta, this has the taste of home-made.

SHORTCUT FOCACCIA:

Brush 2 teaspoons olive oil over purchased Focaccia bread. Sprinkle with ¼ cup finely chopped olives,

2 tablespoons chopped fresh OR 2 teaspoons dried rosemary, and 2 tablespoons fresh parmesan cheese.

Broil until cheese melts.

Harvest Moon or Full Corn Moon?

As a child I would hear adults refer to the Harvest moon, but was too young to understand harvest time and the relationship to the moon. I do remember my grandfather saying the Harvest Moon wasn't really bigger, or more pumpkin-colored than other moons, but was special, which made me think of the song, "Shine on, Shine on Harvest Moon".

Growing up on a small farm, "the harvest" was something mentioned by my father and grandfather, usually around the dinner table. It wasn't until I was older that I found out more about it and what the moons in September and October meant to farmers years ago.

Here is an excerpt from my grandparent's favorite magazine (Farmers' Almanac) that I found "illuminating":

"In Autumn, we celebrate the **Harvest Moon**, which is the full Moon nearest the autumnal equinox. It is also known as the **Full Corn Moon** as it historically has corresponded with the time of harvesting corn. It can occur in September or October and is bright enough to allow finishing all the harvest chores. In the days before tractor lights, the lamp of the Harvest Moon helped farmers bring in crops. As the sun's light faded in the west, the moon would soon rise in the east to illuminate the fields throughout the night." * *"*The Farmer's Almanac Magazine*"

COUNTRY STYLE CORN PUDDING

Preheat oven to 375 degrees

INGREDIENTS: *2 eggs*
½ cup butter, melted
1 (16 ounce) can whole kernel corn, drained
1 cup sour cream
1 (16 ounce) can cream style corn
1 (9 ounce) box corn muffin mix

Beat eggs, add melted butter and blend. Add remaining ingredients, mix well. Pour into a buttered 13x9x2 inch baking dish. Bake for 35-40 minutes, until lightly browned; great with roast pork or chicken, and baked ham.

SUMMER PARTIES

Summer always brings parties and family get-togethers; whether a bridal or babies shower, birthday or anniversary party, sometimes you want to make it special. My sister Laraine did that when she hosted several family get-togethers at her home in Conway New Hampshire. Often, we were there for a mini-reunion to celebrate three August birthdays, and enjoy horseshoes and midnight swims on the Saco River. As casual as it was, Laraine brought it up a notch by serving this sherbet punch which was absolutely refreshing on those hot summer days. Occasionally it was served in a punch bowl, other times in a big pot with a soup ladle, always delicious.

When making for a bridal shower, float large chunks of pastel lime sherbet in a punch bowl and serve in small punch cups; it is very pretty.

LIME SHERBET PUNCH, ORIGINAL RECIPE 1980'S

INGREDIENTS: *3 (half-gallon size) containers lime sherbet (adjust amount to present day ice cream container sizes)*
1 (12 ounce) container frozen lemonade concentrate
1 (2 liter) bottle sprite or 7-up, cold
Vodka to taste **

Spoon slightly softened sherbet, keeping in large chunks, into serving bowl. Pour in thawed concentrate, cold soda, and stir gently to mix. Add vodka, amount as desired. Serve immediately before sherbet melts too much.

**For non-alcoholic version, replace vodka with same amount soda.

FAMILY REUNIONS

JACKMAN Family; banner says it all

Sharing my Family reunion with you; Tips to plan yours.

Every five or six years our immediate family, along with children, pets, and friends (forty to fifty people).meet to just enjoy being together once again.

On a July 4th long weekend we gathered at my sister's home in the White Mountains of New Hampshire for the event which had been scheduled for over a year. Some made a vacation out of it, renting a house close by the week before the reunion.

There were three generations represented, ten kids in the 3rd generation ranging from 3 months to 16 years. We remember the reunions of <u>our</u> youth when we laughed and played with our cousins, and created strong bonds that last to this day. We want the same for this group as well, so we are committed to the next reunion.

With all family reunions it is essential to have a coordinator or two. This year it was my sister and Mike. For about a year, they planned and designated. They are both organized and detail-oriented. Since this was a four day event, lodging was a big issue, as most people were coming from four hours away, as well as others from Cape Cod, Virginia, and Kansas.

<u>Activities:</u> Laraine organized games for the children with small prizes. Mike arranged a special "construction site" area for the little ones, with trucks, sand, gravel and lumber for roads. How great! A story-teller came for an hour one afternoon which provided some rest in the shade. There were "big wheels" to ride, as well as bikes (found in yard sales), and water pistol fights and water balloons that kept us all cool (even those who didn't intend on getting wet). There were family trivia questions (who could answer first, got quite competitive), and a game of "pitch" (cards) going on all weekend. Something for everyone is the plan.

<u>Food:</u> Friday night launched the event with a catered Lobster dinner, a special treat from Laraine and Mike. Guests brought salads and desserts. The "main ingredient" of a reunion is people bringing their traditional favorites, from homemade candies, a pan of cheesecake squares, or a pot of chicken chili. Two of my nieces chose to make and bring dishes that were their Grandmother's original recipes, heartwarming! For several generations we have always had a pot of home- baked beans at our reunions. I made four pounds, using my mother's recipe, and they tasted good, but I can never get them to come out as good as hers. Why is that?

Two things that were great ideas! **A wine station** set up for the weekend, away from the kitchen. Laraine designated her daughter to keep it stocked and glasses clean. Janine and her husband chose an assortment of California and Argentina wines (since Brother Bill lives in Buenos Aries).

Secondly, a **Keurig station** set up on the deck for the entire weekend. Paul was designated to keep it stocked with coffee, tea, and hot chocolate as well as clean mugs, and coffee creamer on ice. With both of these, we never had to stop and make a pot of coffee, or serve wine; tremendous timesavers especially for morning when people were up at different times.

We were lucky to have another niece and her husband who own a local and very professional recycling business. They set up receptacles for bottles, cans, and compost. You might not "have someone in the family", but setting up receptacles outside for everyone to use will make cleanup quicker.

Family Roots/Lineage:

Many families have at least one amateur historian or genealogist. We are fortunate to have had our family lineage done many years ago. Our "line" has been traced back to coming from England in 1624, landing in the port of Newbury Massachusetts. We also have a Family Bible that we are entering data in from the 7th generation of Jackmans. This bible comes to weddings and family gatherings so that newly married and new parents can enter the data themselves. It's a special feeling when one does this. You see and feel what has come before you, and what you are a part of. While at the reunion in 2010 my nephew Steve and his wife entered their first daughter born three months before.

According to a hundred year old Boston Company that repairs bindings of old Bibles and books, our Family Bible is a treasure; printed some-time in the 1870's, a gift to my grandparents at some point after their marriage in 1905.

Reunion Mementos:

Gift bags with an assortment of goodies had our family name on them, and Steve and Kellie brought "beverage can/bottle cozies", cute and useful, imprinted with our family name.

If someone has a video camera, record the event, it will be fun to watch at the next reunion. Try to interview older family members about family history, making up a few questions for them ahead of time; often very interesting and special.

A recipe from our Family Reunion:

Stella Jackman's 70 year antique bowl

MIKE'S SWEET AND WHITE POTATO SALAD

Never having sweet potatoes in potato salad, I was impressed and am a die-hard convert. The green olives were a tasty addition and the salad was gone quickly, sign of a good recipe. There is no written recipe; one of Mike's customers verbally told him how to make it.

Keeping it simple, here are the directions:

Whatever amount you want to make, use one-third red potatoes, one-third Yukon gold potatoes, and one-third sweet potatoes. Cook sweet potatoes separately, unpeeled, watching carefully that they don't' over-cook, as they turn to mush quickly if too soft. Cook remaining potatoes together, also unpeeled, till tender. When cooled to room temperature, peel and cut-up potatoes near the same size, not too small. Place in a large mixing bowl. Add stuffed green olives cut in half, amount to your liking. Add finely chopped onion (1 medium to about 2 pounds of potatoes).

Add mayonnaise of your choice till lightly coated; Season with salt and fresh ground pepper to taste. Spoon into a serving bowl and garnish with several stuffed olives if desired.

Note: (Serving bowl (more than 70 years
old) a favorite of my mother's)

Beloved Neighbor of 50 Years; A Fifth Generation Recipe

I grew up in the small town of Southboro Massachusetts where my family resided from 1941 to 1983. I frequently stop in to see one of our neighbors who remains in her home next to our old homestead. At the time I am writing this she just celebrated her 94th birthday. Martha's parents moved to Southboro in 1925. She and her husband raised their three children, Cliff, Bill, and Ginny, in the same house she remains in today. My mother and Martha became friends as they raised their children over the years. Martha's son Cliff became life-long friends with my brothers Ed and Dick, and Ginny was my sister Susan's true best friend. One of my fondest memories is when Martha would invite my brothers, sisters and I (I was about 10), down to her house on very hot days in the summer to make homemade root beer. We would help her bottle it and put the caps on. To this day I remember how cold and "fizzy" that root beer was. She tells me she still has the bottle caps and the capper.

We love to get together and talk about those years. She fondly remembers all the trouble that my brother Ed and her son Cliff would get into as boys. She laughs as she remembers them hiding behind the stone wall (that separated both properties) while both fathers searched the neighborhood for them (screamed for them is more like it).

Martha shared this particular recipe with me because it has become a huge Templeman family favorite that has lived on through five generations. It is one of her personal favorites as her father brought this old Pennsylvania Dutch recipe with him (tucked into his shirt pocket she says) when he came to Massachusetts from Pennsylvania, which says to her that it must have been his favorite as well.

Martha plants tomatoes each year especially for this dish; "picked fresh from the garden makes these stuffed tomatoes most delicious" she reminds me.

MARTHA'S BAKED STUFFED TOMATOES

Beloved Neighbor in Southboro, MA with home-grown tomatoes

INGREDIENTS: *4 large tomatoes*
1 to 1and 1/4 pounds ground beef
1 medium onion, chopped
1 medium green pepper, chopped
1 stalk celery, chopped
1 teaspoon Italian seasoning, (See Chapter 9 to make
*   your own)*
Salt and pepper to taste

Cut top/stems out of tomatoes, remove and save pulp. Sauté hamburger, add remainder of ingredients including tomato pulp. Simmer all until the pulp is soft. Stuff each tomato. Pour any juices around the tomatoes;

Bake at 350 degrees until tomatoes are soft (30 to 40minutes); sprinkle with grated parmesan cheese, or any grated cheese of your choice. Return to oven for few minutes to melt cheese. Serves 4

CHAPTER 3
HOLIDAYS & EVENTS, NEW YEAR'S TO CHRISTMAS

POPPY STRAWBERRY PIE

BUTTERMILK FRIED CHICKEN

TEXAS CAVIAR DIP

WHOOPIE PIES

REFRESHING WATERMELON

HONEY RAISIN BAKED APPLES

APPLE HONEY CAKE

JIGGLY PUMPKINS

PUMPKIN PANCAKES

BREAD PUDDING BAKED
    IN A PUMPKIN

CANDIED SWEET POTATOES

BAKED INDIAN PUDDING

PUMPKIN SOUP WITH
    CURRYAND MUSHROOMS

CRANBERRY CHUTNEY

OYSTER STUFFING

"TURKEY TERRIFIC" PITA
    SANDWICHES

STANDING RIB ROAST WITH
    ROAST POTATOES

SHITAKE MUSHROOM GRAVY

PEPPERMINT BARK

GINGERBREAD COOKIE CUTOUTS

PECAN PIE COOKIE BARS

SWEET POTATO SCALLION LATKES

JANUARY: NEW YEARS — FAVORITE WAY TO SPEND NEW YEAR'S DAY

Ring out the old, Ring in the New,
Ring happy bells across the snow,
The year is going, let him go,
Ring out the false, ring in the true.

— TENNYSON

Some years this is a do-nothing Holiday after a festive New Year's Eve, or it could be the day to take down the Christmas tree and put away decorations (not my personal favorite).

My best way to spend New Year's Day is to host a Brunch, or be invited to one. It's a wonderful way to celebrate the beginning of a new year.

My Brunch started with about twelve people invited from 11 a.m. to

6 p.m., at times inching up to twenty people, with a few close friends coming early to watch the Tournament of Roses parade. Everyone helps with the preparations and guests bring anything from muffins, coffee cakes, and fruit salads, to a surprise or two, like lobster mac "n" cheese one year, shrimp salad another year.

We would make time for a toast when we each expressed our hope's or wishes for the coming year.

Following are recipes you may want to make whether you are having a "do nothing" day, cooking dinner for your family, or hosting a Brunch.

Easy and qui ck with very little preparation, this ham is delicious.

CIDER GLAZED HAM

Preheat oven to 325 degrees.

INGREDIENTS: *1 fully cooked ham of your choice (I prefer shank end, bone-in, about 5 pounds)*
12 whole cloves
1 cup firmly packed brown sugar
3 and ½ teaspoons dry mustard
1/3 cup apple cider

With a sharp knife, score top of ham; insert cloves. Place in shallow roasting pan. Bake uncovered for 1 and 1/2 hours. Meanwhile, in a small bowl, combine remaining ingredients. Remove ham from oven and spoon glaze over ham. Return it to oven for another 30to45 minutes to continue baking.

This hash is one of the most requested recipes at a Bed & Breakfast in New Plymouth, Ohio called Ravenwood Castle. I found it years ago in a magazine that did a story on several B & B's, sharing a few of their popular recipes. Best of all you can make this ahead, keep refrigerated, and bake an hour before serving.

Royal Breakfast Hash

INGREDIENTS: *5 cups frozen loose-pack, hash brown potatoes, thawed*
1 (10 ¾ ounce) condensed cream of chicken soup
½ cup sour cream
1 cup finely chopped cooked corned beef (can find at deli)
1/3 cup finely chopped onion
1/3 cup finely chopped pepper
1 cup shredded cheddar cheese (4 ounces)
Paprika

Spread potatoes over the bottom of a greased 8x8x2 inch baking dish. In a medium bowl, combine soup, sour cream, corned beef, onion, and green pepper. Spread over potatoes. Bake uncovered in a 350 degree oven for 40 to 45 minutes or until bubbly and top begins to brown. Sprinkle with cheese and paprika just before serving, returning to oven for a few minutes just to melt cheese. Makes 4-6 servings.

GLAZED FRUIT

For glaze, combine 1 cup sugar, 2 tablespoons cornstarch, and 2 cups of orange juice in a small saucepan. Over medium heat, stir until smooth; bring to a boil, continuing to stir for 2 minutes or until thickened. Put in a bowl, cover and chill for 2 hours.

In a large serving bowl, combine 3 cups cubed honeydew melon, 3 medium firm bananas, sliced, 2 cups of green grapes, and 2 cups halved fresh strawberries. Add cooled glaze and gently toss to coat. Makes 10 servings.

February

Super Bowl Sunday   A Day for Football, Family, Friends, and Food

We are definitely a football-loving family. My father started it all by playing football for his high school team, which culminated in his being recruited by a local college with a full scholarship. Two out of my four brothers played for their high school teams and several of my nephews played football or rugby. There is no doubt Super Bowl Sunday is big in my family.

Taking place in early February, this event has become a reason to give parties of all types and sizes. At the very least it has become a good reason for simply getting together for fun and food. No food is out of bounds, anything goes, everything goes, burgers, fries, chili, pasta, pizza, and almost any kind of bean dip and cheese dip. Advice from my brother, Richard is to keep the food simple and quick so that one can stay in front of the TV for pre-game, game and half-time (not to miss the Super Bowl commercials).

Tradition can play a big role here, from my brother Bill's Bean Dip, or my nephew Ed's "Attack 6 Chili "or Eric's Buffalo Chicken dip, all annual favorites served while watching the Superbowl games with pride.

Jack's Story: "Attack 6" War Winning Chili

Quite the guy Jack is, a West Point graduate, Army Major with two tours (one in Iraq and one in Afghanistan), a medical school graduate now with M.D. after his name, and beloved husband of Pam and daughter

Kaylin, as well as Daddy to 2 year-old daughter, Callie Brynn, and with much pride, my nephew.

Here's the story behind Jack's chili recipe in his words:

"I call the chili "Attack 6" because ATTACK SIX was my radio call sign when I was a commander in the 3rd Infantry Division (mechanized) at Fort Stewart, Georgia when I first made my own chili…hence my claim of not AWARD winning chili but "WAR winning chili". My favorite batch, not necessarily the best tasting, was made in Iraq, in 2006 when I commanded a detachment of special operations warriors fighting in Al Anbar province Iraq. We had to pull some big favors to get some of the ingredients needed for the chili at our Task Force compound outside of Ramadi, Iraq. The current version (with the beer) was taste-tested by a group of my fellow physicians during my residency training one fall sitting in front of a Patriots football game and it got rave reviews! I don't remember where I got the recipe for the cornbread, I was never a fan of plain cornbread and this version adds a sweet and spicy element that enhances the chili."

With Love,
Edward C. "Jack" Jackman, MD

ATTACK 6 WAR-WINNING CHILI

INGREDIENTS: *1 tablespoon olive oil*
2 (16 ounce) packages "Johnsonville" brand, sausage links: 1 package sweet, 1 package hot.
1 (12 ounce) package Apple wood smoked bacon diced into small pieces.
1 large white onion, diced

1 large red bell pepper, diced

2 medium red chili peppers, cut off ends, halve length-
wise, slice ¼ inch thick

2 medium jalapeno peppers, cut off ends, halve length-
wise, slice ¼ inch thick

3 cloves garlic, minced

3 tablespoons chili powder

1 teaspoon cumin

1(12 ounce) bottle Samuel Adams chocolate bock beer
(or other dark beer)

(Note: I could not find chocolate bock beer, but substi-
tuted with a chocolate stout beer)

1 (28 ounce) can crushed tomatoes

3 tablespoons tomato paste

1 ½ cups fresh or frozen corn

1 (16 ounce) can black beans, rinsed and drained

1 (16 ounce) can red kidney beans, rinsed and drained

In a large skillet fry diced bacon until soft and fat begins to render. Add bacon and bacon fat to a large cooking pot. Remove casings from sausage and break into pieces. Add to same skillet and sauté until no longer pink. Use a wooden spoon to crumble sausage as it cooks. Stir in onion, red bell pepper, hot peppers, garlic, chili powder and cumin. Continue cooking until the onion softens, about 5 minutes. Add the beer and allow all to simmer for 5to10 minutes. Add to the large pot. Stir in the tomatoes, tomato paste and cook uncovered for 20 to30 minutes on medium low, stirring occasionally. Taste and adjust seasonings with salt and pepper. Stir in beans and corn. Bring all to a simmer and cook an additional 20to30 minutes. Transfer to a crock pot and let cook on low for several hours.

Serve with corn chips, sour cream, shredded Mexican cheese, and the following cornbread.

HAPPY JACK'S MEXICAN CORNBREAD

Preheat oven to 350 degrees

INGREDIENTS: *1 cup all purpose cornmeal*
½ cup all purpose flour
2 tablespoons baking powder
2/3 cup milk
2 eggs, lightly beaten
1/3 cup vegetable oil
3 tablespoons sugar
½ teaspoon salt
½ cup chopped onion
1 (14 ounce) can creamed corn
1 cup grated cheddar jack cheese
¾ cups chopped hot peppers (3 medium jalapeno and 3 medium green chilies)

Butter well an 8 or 9 inch square baking pan.

In a large bowl combine cornmeal, flour, baking powder, milk, eggs, oil, salt, and sugar. Combine well, do not over mix. Stir in onion and corn. Pour half of batter into prepared pan; sprinkle cheese and peppers uniformly over batter. Cover with remaining batter. Bake for 35 minutes or until golden brown and toothpick inserted in center comes out clean.

Have a Party; Game Day Snacking

This Buffalo Chicken Dip recipe is like hot wings all wrapped up in a cheesy dip. It has become a classic over the years and very popular, the hotter the better! My niece Tracy and her husband Eric sent me their version which I am passing on along with their note:

"Eric first tried a chicken dip at one of our friend's parties and really enjoyed it. He has always loved buffalo chicken and different dips, so combining the two was genius. After the party, he went home and searched online for an easy buffalo chicken dip. He chose one from several different versions and whipped up his own version. He never serves it with celery or crackers. Eric's two "must have's" when he serves this dip; Tostitos brand "scoops" and Frank's Red Hot sauce, and plenty of it. This has been a hit when we've had parties and is always tasty on Sundays when we watch football. Eric & Tracy

Buffalo Chicken Dip

Makes about 5 cups

INGREDIENTS: *2 (10 ounce) cans chunk chicken, drained*
                    2 (8 ounce) packages cream cheese, softened
                    1 cup bottled ranch dressing
                    ¾ cup pepper sauce (suggest Frank's Red Hot brand)
                    1 and ½ cups shredded cheddar cheese

Suggested accompaniments: celery sticks and chicken-flavored crackers.

Directions: Heat chicken and hot sauce in a skillet over medium heat until heated through. Stir in cream cheese and ranch dressing continuing to stir until well blended and warm. Mix in half of the shredded cheese and transfer the mixture to a slow cooker. Sprinkle the remaining cheese over the top, cover and cook on low setting until hot and bubbly. Share it!

Note: To cook in the oven, mix all ingredients together until smooth and place in an ovenproof dish and bake at 350 degrees until hot, about 25 minutes.

It was sometime in the 1980's when my brother Bill started bringing the following dip to our family get-togethers at our parent's home on Cape Cod. Prior to that Bill remembers this Tex-Mex style dip popular among US Army families entertaining around the world during the 1970's and 80's.

BILL JACKMAN'S LAYERED BEAN DIP

Serves 4 to 6

INGREDIENTS: *1 can refried beans*
½ to 1 package dry TACO seasoning
4 large or 6 small avocados, mashed
2 teaspoons lemon juice
1 (16 ounce) container sour cream
2 to 3 cups shredded cheddar cheese
½ jar green olives, halved (pimento-stuffed green olives provide color)
Side dish of jalapeno pepper rings, large bag of tortilla chips

Use a 2 inch deep serving dish. Mix refried beans with Taco seasoning mix to your taste, spread on bottom of serving dish. Mix lemon juice with mashed avocados and spread over the beans. Spread sour cream over all. Top with cheddar cheese. Sprinkle on green olives. Cover and keep chilled.

Hot & Honeyed Chicken Wings

These are addictive; bet you can't eat just one!

Preheat oven to 400 degrees.

INGREDIENTS: *3 pounds chicken wings (approximately 16 wings)*
¾ cup salsa, not too chunky – choose your "heat"; mild,
medium, or hot
2/3 cup honey
1/3 cup soy sauce
¼ cup Dijon mustard
½ teaspoon ground ginger

Cut off and discard wing tips; cut each wing in half at joint. Mix all ingredients in a large bowl; add wings and coat well. Place wings in a single layer on a foil-lined 15 x 10 inch shallow pan; lightly season with salt and pepper. Bake for 55 minutes or till browned. Turn if needed. Brush with sauce last half hour of cooking.

Valentine's Day: I Have Always Loved It

What a wonderful celebration someone tucked into the middle of winter; February, a cold and sometimes very snowy month. And voila, we have this day of red hearts, candy, flowers, and so much more depending upon your age (could be lace and satin on a nightgown). And this day is not just for lovers out there, it is for anyone who has someone to love; grandparent, grandchild, son, daughter, dad, mom, and on and on.

I think I became a romantic in the third grade, receiving those paper valentine hearts that you write out the night before and pass out to everyone in your class, writing something special to that boy you have your first crush on.

I melt over vintage cards, pretty flowers, pink and lace, and handwritten notes. I have three boys, who when young could have done without some of the mushy cards and homemade hearts, but they were troopers, and as grown men today, like and laugh at the memories of heart-shaped pancakes and finding red balloons tied to their chairs on Valentine's morning. They know it was all out of love.

Valentine's Day can be simple. I am motivated by a recent television ad where a woman presents a wrapped valentine chocolate to the people she meets in her day; coffee shop waitress, grocery store check-out, bank teller. She gives out a chocolate and a smile, quick wave, and she's off, leaving happy people in her wake.

So I say, make a cold winter day fun and HEART warming for yourself and others.

IDEAS AND TIPS

Strawberries stuffed with lightly-sweetened cream cheese and walnuts are perfect for that romantic evening; goes great with champagne.

Make a red velvet cake, and frost with a rich chocolate frosting; top with candy hearts, candy kisses, or x's and o's.

What you write in a Valentine's card can be as meaningful as the card itself. Think of two happy moments you have shared with your special someone this year and mention them in the card.

Write thirty messages of love and leave all around the house to be found during the month.

Take a walk together and hold hands.

Write a few "coupons to collect" for items such as a neck massage or ten minute backrub.

If you and a few of your friends enjoy crafts, invite them to a "craft-making party".

Spend an afternoon with red construction paper, and white lace paper and make your own valentines for your family. Include red punch, finger foods, valentine cookies and chocolates to complete an enjoyable day.

For your Neighbors: Cooking or baking for people you care about remains one of the oldest ways to say "I'm thinking of you". Sweet treats are for Valentine's Day, but don't limit yourself. For instance, my friends and family almost fall to my feet when I bake homemade bread for them.

February is HEART MONTH. Be good to your own heart; de-stress with a good book, take a leisurely walk, light more candles around the house, pamper yourself and make the entire month one of love for yourself as well as others.

SWEETS: Chocolate cookies are dipped in white chocolate and made special for Valentine's Day by using a heart-shaped cookie cutter.

White Chocolate-Dipped Heart Cookies

INGREDIENTS: *1 cup butter, softened*
½ cup sugar
1 teaspoon vanilla extract
2 cups all-purpose flour
¼ cup baking cocoa
1 cup white chocolate chips

2 tablespoons heavy cream, divided
½ cup semisweet chocolate chips

In a small mixing bowl, cream butter and sugar; beat in vanilla. Combine the flour and cocoa; gradually add to creamed mixture. On a lightly floured surface, roll out dough to one-quarter inch thickness. Cut with a 3-inch heart shaped cookie cutter. Place 2 inches apart on ungreased baking sheet. Bake at 375 degrees for 8 to 10 minutes or until firm. Remove to wire racks to cool.

In a microwave-safe bowl, heat white chocolate chips and 1 tablespoon cream until melted, stirring frequently. Dip both sides of cookies into melted mixture. Let harden on waxed paper or parchment paper.

In another microwave-safe bowl, heat dark chocolate chips with 1 tablespoon cream, stirring frequently. Drizzle lightly across each cookie in several lines (thin with more cream if necessary).

TRIPLE CHOCOLATE KISSES

Crisp Meringue Cookies with a Chocolate Kiss Center. These look like they would take a lot of time to make, but not so. Makes approximately 3 ½ dozen

INGREDIENTS: *2 egg whites*
¼ teaspoon cream of tartar
½ cup sugar
¼ teaspoon almond extract
1 square (1 ounce) semisweet chocolate, grated
42 milk chocolate candy kisses
baking cocoa for dusting

In a mixing bowl, beat egg whites until foamy. Add cream of tartar; beat until soft peaks form, about 6 minutes. Gradually add sugar, beating until stiff peaks form, about 5-6 minutes. Beat in extract. Gently fold in grated chocolate. Insert a medium open-star tip in a pastry bag (or plastic bag). Fill with meringue. On lightly greased baking sheets, pipe forty-two 1 inch circles. Press a chocolate kiss into the center of each. Pipe meringue around each kiss in continuous circles from the base to the top until kiss is completely covered. Lightly dust with cocoa.

Bake in a pre-heated 325 degree oven for 15-18 minutes or until edges are lightly browned; immediately remove to wire racks to cool.

Molded RED HOT Hearts (Fun for children.)

Using cinnamon candies we call "RED HOTS", the kids will think you are very cool!

INGREDIENTS: *¼ cup red-hot cinnamon candies*
Scant 1 cup boiling water (just a bit less than a full cup)
1 package (3 ounce) strawberry or raspberry gelatin
2 and ¼ cups applesauce

In a bowl, dissolve candies in the water. Stir in gelatin until well dissolved. Fold in applesauce. Pour into 12 lightly oiled 1/3 cup individual heart molds OR a 4-cup heart-shaped mold OR onto a baking sheet with at least a half-inch rim. If baking sheet is used, cut individual servings with a heart-shaped cookie cutter.

Heartfelt Cakes for your Sweetheart

Strawberry Heart Cake

Need 2 waxed paper-lined 8 inch cake pans, one square and one round.

INGREDIENTS: *1 package (18 ¼ ounce) white cake mix*
1 package (3 ounce) strawberry gelatin
3 tablespoons all-purpose flour
1/3 cup vegetable oil
4 eggs
1 package (10 ounce) frozen sweetened strawberries, thawed
½ cup cold water
½ cup butter, softened
5 to 5 ½ cups confectioners' sugar
Red-hot candies, optional

In a mixing bowl, combine cake mix, gelatin and flour. Beat in oil and eggs. Drain strawberries, reserving ½ cup syrup for frosting. Add berries and water to batter, mix well. Divide batter between the two prepared cake pans.

Bake at 350 degrees for 30 to 35 minutes (square) and 35 to 40 minutes (round) or until toothpick inserted near center comes out dry. Cool for 10 minutes; remove from pans to wire racks to cool completely.

In a small mixing bowl, combine soft butter and reserved syrup. Gradually add confectioners' sugar; beat until light and fluffy, about 2 minutes. Place square cake diagonally on a 20"x15" board that has been covered with red paper. Cut round cake in half. Frost each cut side; place frosted sides against the top two sides of the square cake, forming a heart; frost rest of the cake. Decorate with red-hots, candy hearts, or serve as is.

Chocolate Fudge Cake with Chocolate Frosting

This cake is simple to make as it starts with a boxed mix. It is quick enough to put together to be a nice surprise for a supper dessert, a treat for a helpful neighbor, or a special addition to a Valentine party. I used a disposable heart-shaped baking pan that I found in a large craft store, and the next day made a few cupcakes with the left-over batter.

Preheat oven to 325 degrees;

CAKE INGREDIENTS: *1 box Devil's Food Cake mix*
1 (3.4 ounce) package chocolate pudding mix
3 large eggs
1 teaspoon vanilla
½ cup vegetable or canola oil
1 and 1/3 cups water
½ to 1 cup dark chocolate chips, amount based on personal preference, Optional

Grease and flour 13x9 inch baking pan or heart-shaped pan

Combine cake mix, pudding mix, eggs, vanilla, oil and water in a large mixing bowl. Beat at medium speed for 2 minutes. Stir in chocolate chips. Pour into pan. Bake for 35 to 40 minutes or until toothpick inserted in center comes out clean. Cool in pan. Frosting is optional. If desired, decorate with a light dusting of confectioners' sugar.

NOTE: If you are baking cake in a heart-shaped pan, fill pan two-thirds full with batter and bake at 325 degrees for 60 minutes, depending on pan size. Use toothpick in center to test if done. Make cupcakes with leftover batter if desired.

Rich Chocolate Frosting

Heat ½ pint of heavy cream just to beginning of a boil. Using 10 and ½ ounces semisweet chocolate break into pieces and add to cream and stir until melted. Let cool, and chill for 30 minutes, then whisk until thickened to a spreadable consistency.

MALTED HOT CHOCOLATE

This hot chocolate goes with the cake spectacularly, particularly because Valentine's Day comes in a cold month and this would be a "mug of warmth", welcomed by many. Top it off with whipped cream and crushed malted milk balls. Makes 4 to 6 Servings.

INGREDIENTS: *2 cups half and half*
1 (4 ounce) bar semisweet chocolate, chopped
4 cups milk
¼ cup sugar
1 tablespoon vanilla extract
2 cups malted milk powder (find in baking aisle of supermarket)
Garnish: whipped cream, chopped malted milk balls.

In a large saucepan, combine half and half and chocolate over medium heat, whisking constantly until chocolate has melted. Add milk, sugar, and vanilla, whisking until sugar is dissolved. Bring to a simmer, stirring frequently, do not boil. Whisk in malted milk powder until smooth. Pour into mugs. Garnish with whipped cream and candy if desired.

March: Maple Syrup Season in New England

As Winter Leaves us, Trees Come to Life with Syrup

"Sap gathering" begins. This is the process of collecting sap from maple trees and boiling it down to make maple syrup. It is a way of life, passed down through generations in many families. Referred to as "sugar-makers", they are proud people dedicated to producing the highest quality maple syrup. Timing is everything, with Mother Nature in control. Tapping (inserting taps into tree trunks) too early or too late can alter the quantity/quality of the finished syrup. "Sugaring off" as it is known, starts in late February and runs through March. The watery sap starts flowing when the temperatures rise above freezing during the day, and fall below at night. The greater the temperature fluctuates, the faster the sap flows. Once the trees thaw, the sap stops running. An average maple tree provides ten gallons of sap each spring. As it is boiled down, the water boils away, leaving sweet syrup. It takes about forty gallons of sap to make one gallon of maple syrup; nothing is added.

If you ever have the chance, visit a Sugarhouse where maple syrup is made. Listen to the stories of the sugar- makers, some continuing a lifestyle that began generations ago. I could feel and see the dedication and caring for this age-old tradition with deep desires to not see it fade away. Watch the whole process and be awed with all the products that can be made with maple syrup.

Tips:

1. Always refrigerate maple syrup after opening.

2. Can be frozen; freeze and thaw any number of times.

Bacon Wrapped Scallops

Skewer scallop on toothpick; wrap ½ piece of bacon around it, brush with maple syrup, broil until browned and "sizzly."

MAPLE-GLAZED PARSNIPS

INGREDIENTS: *2 pounds parsnips, peeled, quartered lengthwise, cut into 2 inch pieces.*
4 tablespoons butter
¼ cup mustard seeds
3 tablespoons pure maple syrup
2 tablespoons Dijon mustard

Steam parsnips over medium heat until tender, about 10 minutes. Drain on paper towel.

Melt 1 tablespoon butter in a small skillet over low heat. Add mustard seeds; cover and cook until beginning to pop, about 2 minutes. Remove from heat. Let stand until popping stops, about 8 minutes.

Melt remaining butter in a large nonstick skillet over medium heat. Stir in maple syrup and Dijon mustard. Add parsnips; toss to coat. Sauté until parsnips are glazed, about 10 minutes. Add mustard seeds and toss to coat;

Season to taste with salt and pepper. Makes 4-6 servings Note: This is excellent with Roast Pork

Maple Bran Muffins

Preheat oven to 400 degrees

INGREDIENTS: *1 cup all-purpose flour*
1 cup bran flakes
1 teaspoon baking soda
1/2 cup raisins
1/4 cup chopped walnuts
1 cup nonfat sour cream or light version
1 cup pure maple syrup
1 egg
1 egg white

Spray large muffin tins with nonstick oil. Combine flour, bran flakes, and baking soda in a large bowl. Stir in raisins and walnuts. In a separate bowl, beat together sour cream, syrup, and eggs. Pour liquid into flour mixture and mix for 20 seconds, till all is moistened (try not to over mix). Fill muffin cups 2/3 full. Bake for 20 minutes or till toothpick inserted into center of muffin comes out clean. Makes 12 lowfat muffins.

St. Patrick's Day: Classic Dessert from the 1970s

Watergate Salad made its debut around 1974 and quickly became popular nationwide. "Kraft" Company had just developed a new instant pudding flavor, pistachio, and this recipe was developed using the pudding as its main ingredient. The pistachio flavor was a hit, and everywhere you went people were serving this. How could you go wrong with pudding, marshmallows, pecans, and crushed pineapple?

In 2005 the Kraft Company re-published the recipe along with some research on how the dessert got its name. According to the website, it derived its name either for WATERGATE (Nixon era), or the WATERGATE HOTEL in Washington DC, newly built at that time. At this point we may never know exactly how it was named. WATERGATE and a salad at that, but the main thing is this is really good and makes a very pretty and impressive dessert to serve. Because the pistachio pudding tints the dessert a pastel green it has become popular to serve on St. Patrick's Day.

WATERGATE SALAD

INGREDIENTS: *1 package pistachio instant pudding mix (4 serving size)*
1 (20 ounce) can crushed pineapple in juice, undrained
1 cup miniature marshmallows
½ cup chopped pecans
1 and ½ cups whipped topping, such as cool whip brand
Optional topping: additional whipped cream and chopped pecans

Mix dry pudding mix, pineapple with juice, marshmallows, and half a cup of pecans in a large bowl until well blended. Gently stir in whipped topping. Cover and refrigerate. Serves 4

This is very attractive served in a see-through glass bowl, topped with fresh whipped cream and a sprinkle of chopped pecans.

A BIT O' GREEN CAKE AND IRISH "HAPPY"

To write a column on St. Patrick's Day one year, I wanted as much of the real thing from somebody who was Irish; perhaps favorite foods of the day, traditions they follow, what it means to them to be Irish; authenticity is what I was looking for.

I immediately thought of my Cousin Lee's wife, Sue, whom I had been talking too recently about her Irish ancestry, deep Irish pride, and that St. Patrick's Day is a favorite time for her.

Sue and Lee Jackman have lived all their lives in Fitchburg Massachusetts. They met, married and raised their family there. Sue's maiden name is "Dower"; an old Gaelic family name. Irish is considered one of the important ancestries in Fitchburg, with a fascinating history of its own.

When Sue speaks of Irish pride, it's her grandfather that is foremost in her mind and memories.

Sue's Grandfather's name was "Happy" Dower, called that most all his life she states, saying literally he was happy all the time, and the name stuck. According to memory and family artifacts, this is some of his story:

"Happy" Dower came to the United States from County Cork, Ireland when he was nearly fifteen years old. It was the early 1900s and Cork was a hotbed of Guerilla fighting, and Happy boarded a ship that would bring him to Fitchburg, which at the time was where factories were being expanded and waves of immigrants came to find work. When he saw Fitchburg for the first time he knew this was where he belonged. For the rest of his life he would often say:

"I came from County Cork, divided by a river, to live here in this city, also divided by a river."

But Happy's life's work was not in the factories, but in the railroad, known as the Fitchburg-Leominster Railway (the old F&L). Happy started by driving Trolley cars, and continued when the city switched to buses, driving for nearly fifty years. A favorite family memory was when Happy Dower would often bust out singing this favorite song;

I've been workin' on the railroad,
All the live long day.
I've been workin' on the railroad,
Just to pass the time away.
Don't you hear the whistle blowing?
Rise up so early in the morn.
Don't you hear the captain shouting
"Dinah, blow your horn?"

A favorite dessert on St. Patrick's Day for Sue and some of Happy Dower's twenty-seven grandchildren was this green jello Poke cake that became popular in the 1950's.

SHAMROCK GREEN CAKE

This is a very moist cake and surprisingly light.

INGREDIENTS: *1 package white cake mix, regular size*
2 packages (3 ounce each) lime gelatin
1 cup boiling water
1/2 cup cold water

TOPPING: *1 cup cold milk*
1 package (3.4 ounce) instant vanilla pudding mix
1 carton (8 ounce) frozen whipped topping, thawed
*** Decorations optional – green food coloring, green/ white candies*

Prepare and bake cake according to package directions, using a greased 13 inch x 9 inch baking dish. Cool on a wire rack for at least 1 hour.

In a small bowl dissolve gelatin in boiling water; stir in cold water and set aside.

With a wooden skewer or end of wooden spoon, poke holes about an inch apart into cooled cake. Slowly pour gelatin over cake. Cover and refrigerate.

In a large bowl whisk milk and pudding mix for 2 minutes (mixture will be thick). Fold in whipped topping; tint frosting green with food coloring, if desired. Decorate with green/white candies as desired. Cover and refrigerate.

Note - Do not poke holes too far apart; pour gelatin over cake very slowly so that it has time to seep in.

April: Passover — Lavish Meals and Beautiful Traditions

An important eight-day celebration which commemorates the freedom of Jewish slaves from Egypt; this is a wonderful time of lavish meals, singing songs, and families gathering together to celebrate beautiful and traditional customs.

I have good memories of this holiday, when as a young nurse, I enjoyed working in a small convalescent home owned by a wonderful Jewish family. I was taught by their fabulous cook some of the details in keeping a kosher kitchen and serving kosher meals. I learned a lot about Passover traditions, and learned respect for those traditions, and each year at this time I look forward to the beauty of this celebration and of course enjoying its traditional food; one of my favorites being matzo enjoyed in many different ways..

In America brisket is a traditional entrée of a Jewish holiday meal. This recipe is *kosher for Passover.*

Serves 8 to 10. Many cooks prefer to make brisket the day before you plan to serve it.

BEEF BRISKET

INGREDIENTS: *3 large onions, thinly sliced*
1 and ½ teaspoons salt
2 bay leaves
2 tablespoons vegetable oil
3 cups homemade or canned beef broth
4 to 5 pound beef brisket
2 sprigs fresh parsley
1 teaspoon freshly cracked black pepper
6 black peppercorns
3 tablespoons matzo cake meal

Convenient herb sack: Place parsley, peppercorns and bay leaves in a 4 inch square of cheesecloth. Tie the ends together with kitchen string; this can be easily removed from the pan when done.

In a small bowl, mix together matzo cake meal, salt, and ground black pepper. Pat this dry rub seasoning on all sides of the meat. In a large nonstick dutch oven or heavy casserole pan, heat the oil over medium-high heat. Brown the meat on all sides, turning as needed (careful when turning to not burn yourself with hot fat). After browning, pour off and discard excess fat. Add the onions, herb sack, and beef stock. Bring to a boil, and then lower the heat so the liquid barely simmers. Cook covered, either on top of the stove or in a preheated oven 325 degrees, for 2 ½ to 3 hours. Turn the meat over when halfway done. Check often to not let the liquid boil.

When cooked and tender, let cool. Refrigerate 6 hours or overnight. Scrape off fat and discard. Slice. Serve with pan juices and white horseradish if desired.

Matzo is a large, flat cracker traditionally eaten during Passover.
When the Israelites made their Exodus from Egypt there was no time
for bread to rise, so matzo (without yeast), symbolizes that journey to
freedom.
Top whole matzo with spreads or cheese. Use ground matzo meal for
making cakes and matzo balls

Swiss Chard Matzo Torte

This recipe is an easy vegetarian meal where matzo, cheeses and swiss
chard is layered lasagna-like. It can be served room temperature or hot.
This recipe can be doubled (use a 9 x 13 pan) and may be frozen.
Preheat oven to 400 degrees

INGREDIENTS: *1 teaspoon olive oil*
1 medium Spanish onion, finely chopped (about 1 cup)
2 garlic cloves, minced
1 small bunch Swiss chard, rinsed thoroughly, discard stems
2 cups part-skim ricotta cheese
2 eggs
½ teaspoon salt
3 whole squares matzos
½ cup crumbled feta cheese
Lightly grease an 8x8 inch pan.

Heat oil in a nonstick skillet over medium-high heat; add onion and
garlic and cook until golden, stirring occasionally, about 7 minutes.
While onion cooks, prepare chard. Remove excess water and finely chop
leaves to get about 4 cups, loosely packed. Add to onion and continue
to cook for 4 minutes until chard is limp but still bright green. Remove
from heat and cool for a few minutes. Place ricotta, eggs, and salt in a

small bowl and mix well. Combine chard mixture with eggs and ricotta mixture and stir until well mixed.

Place 1 matzo in bottom of prepared pan and top with 1 cup of the chard mixture; top with second matzo.

Repeat. There should be about ¼ cup of the chard mixture remaining. Top with third matzo and spread remaining chard mixture on top, then sprinkle with feta cheese. Bake just until golden, about 30 minutes. Serves 4

LEMON CHEESECAKE BARS

Preheat oven to 350 degrees

INGREDIENTS: *1 ½ cups soft coconut macaroon cookie crumbs (may substitute with crushed sugar cookies)*
2 tablespoons margarine, melted
2 (8 ounce) packages cream cheese (Kraft brand offers kosher for Passover)
½ cup white sugar
½ teaspoon grated lemon peel and 1 tablespoon of lemon juice
½ teaspoon imitation vanilla extract
2 eggs

Mix crumbs and margarine; press firmly onto bottom of greased 8 inch square baking pan. Beat softened cream cheese, sugar, lemon peel and juice, and vanilla in a large bowl on medium speed until well blended. Add eggs one at a time, beat just till blended. Pour over crust. Bake for 20 to 25 minutes until center is almost set. Refrigerate 3 hours or overnight. Cut into 16 bars.

Passover Candy Treats

Matzo Blossoms Combine 3 sheets of crumbled matzo with 3 cups of melted chocolate chips and 1 cup each of: dried cherries, slivered almonds, and coconut. Drop by teaspoonfuls onto a baking sheet lined with waxed paper; refrigerate until firm. (May substitute with chopped dates and walnuts with the coconut) *Reese's Pieces Matzo* Arrange 3 and ½ sheets of matzo on a parchment-line baking sheet. Melt ½ cup butter with ½ cup brown sugar, stirring until sugar is dissolved; cook 5 minutes longer. Spread mixture over matzo; bake 5 minutes in a 350 degree oven. Remove and sprinkle with 1 ½ cups semi-sweet chocolate and peanut butter pieces. Let stand 5 minutes to melt; spread melted mixture over matzo. Sprinkle with chopped peanuts.

Refrigerate until firm; Break into large pieces.

EASTER MEMORIES

It's not just Easter Sunday that was special to me, but also the coming of spring. After a gray and cold winter, one couldn't get enough of the warmer, sunnier days and pastel colors everywhere. It was special to shop for just the right new outfit that always included a new dress and hat for the girls in my family, and new ties and shoes for the boys. Going to church on Easter Sunday was definitely an occasion, not only for reflection, but to see the Church with colorful plants everywhere. Of course walking into church with my seven brothers and sisters all dressed up, made me feel proud and special as neighbors and friends would say "here come the Jackman kids".

Every child from two to twelve would walk up to the front of the church and return their UNICEF collection box and receive a flowering plant. It was like watching an indoor Easter Parade! It seemed everything was new; the sunny day, pastel colors of new Easter outfits, flowers galore, and a happy infectious attitude that showed on many faces.

Spring was here!

HOMEMADE CHOCOLATE-COVERED EGGS

I love the rich and fresh taste of homemade candy and these will not disappoint you as they melt in your mouth.

If you choose, decorate finished chocolates using tubes of colored candy-coating.

INGREDIENTS: *¾ cup peanut butter, smooth or chunky*
¼ cup salted butter, room temperature but not overly soft
¼ teaspoon vanilla extract
1 cup fine flaked coconut
½ cup finely chopped pecans or walnuts
1and ½ to 2 cups confectioners' sugar, divided
12 ounces of a good chocolate or 2 cups chocolate chips;
semi-sweet or milk chocolate
2 tablespoons shortening, measured accurately

In a mixing bowl, cream peanut butter, vanilla, and butter until well mixed. Fold in coconut, nuts and 1 cup of the sugar, mixing well. Sprinkle some of the remaining sugar on a board. Turn out mixture onto board; knead in enough of the remaining sugar a little at a time until the mixture holds its shape when formed, using as much confectioners' sugar as you need. Shape into small egg-shaped pieces. Cover with waxed paper and chill for 1 hour. In a double boiler over hot water, melt chocolate and shortening, stirring until smooth. Dip eggs; place on waxed paper to harden. Chill; Makes about 20 small candies.

FAVORITE EASTER CAKE

This bunny cake is the cutest thing, and young children will delight in the fun of decorating it. I first saw this cake in a magazine in the early 1980s. At that time my sons were three and seven years old.

"Simple to make" was the title caption and all I needed to know to try it, along with a picture of the finished and decorated cake. I baked the cake layers and cut one layer into the three pieces that formed the ears and bowtie. After covering with frosting the kids would decide how to decorate it; red or black for the licorice whiskers, gumdrops or jelly beans for the bowtie, perhaps Oreo cookies for the eyes.

For presentation we would place the cake on an oval platter, surround it with Easter "green grass" and marshmallow chicks. We made it every Easter until the boys were "too cool" and no longer children.

I made it about five years ago for a children's event and my then thirty year old son came in and saw it on the kitchen table and said, "that brings back memories". I asked, "You remember it?" He responded,

"Absolutely! We made it every year for Easter and it's a favorite part of my childhood".

So there you go parents, they do remember.

Festive Bunny Cake for Children

You will need:

Two, 8 or 9 inch cake layers, any flavor; I have made yellow, lemon, spice, and white.

White frosting, enough for a 2 layer cake or 13 x 9 inch cake. (On occasion I have used pre-made in the little tubs, thinning with light cream to fluff it).

1 package fresh flaked coconut

Green and red food coloring.

Pieces of thin red string licorice for whiskers and mouth as pictured.

Gum drops for eyes, nose, and bowtie.

Place one cooled cake layer (the face) in the center of a large serving platter. Cut 2nd layer into 3 pieces placing the 2 outer pieces for the ears at the top of the round layer, and the "bowtie" (middle piece) at the bottom of the round layer. Cover entire cake with frosting. Cover all with coconut, saving about 2 tablespoons to tint pink for the center of the ears. Use candy and licorice to make eyes, nose, and whiskers; dot bowtie with gumdrops.

Comments from Wanda H.: *Wow! Thanks for those memories! I used to make the Easter Bunny cake every year for my kids (without coconut, not a family favorite), but it was even earlier than the 80's. I remember making it strawberry flavored one Easter because it was my daughter's favorite.*

Comments from Susan, Atkinson New Hampshire: *I just had to write and tell you how much I enjoyed the Easter Bunny cake. I too found that picture of the cake in a magazine around 1980 and made it every year until recently when my grown children seemed to lose interest! Yet, I recall how annoyed they were the first year I didn't make it!! Well, by next Easter I will have my first grandchild and I have informed them that "BUNNY CAKE" will be back. I always used black shoestring licorice for the whiskers and mouth but that is impossible to find.*

Thank you for a reminder that even old recipes can be revived to brighten any occasion. Still smiling.

MARY'S CINNAMON BUNS

These are wonderful for Easter morning!

If you can't quite recall the last time you made cinnamon buns from scratch, trust me, just waking up to the aroma in your kitchen will be incentive enough.

More than ten years ago I came across this recipe in a magazine that did a feature on Inn recipes, and the Pincushion Mountain B&B in Minnesota was one of several selected to submit a recipe. I called the B&B and spoke to the new owner who states that this recipe was first made by the cook at that time, Mary, who said it originally came from her mother. The cinnamon buns continued to be so popular that Lynn (new owner) says Mary's cinnamon buns (name I gave them) are still made to this day.

Bed & Breakfast establishments are known for great home-made food; and in this recipe extra flavor comes from vanilla cake mix. Since this recipe makes a lot, I like to freeze half for another time. These rolls freeze well for up to 3 months. Makes 32 cinnamon rolls.

TIPS: 1. Warm all ingredients to room temperature

2. Use dental floss to slice through soft rolled dough; it is strong and won't distort the roll.

INGREDIENTS: *1 box (2 layer size) French vanilla cake mix (plain va-*
nilla ok substitute)
5 ½ to 6 cups all-purpose flour
2 packages active dry yeast
1 teaspoon salt
2 ½ cups warm water (120 to 130 degrees)
¼ cup butter, softened
¾ cup granulated sugar
1 tablespoon cinnamon
1 and 1/3 cups packed brown sugar

1 cup butter
2 tablespoons light-colored corn syrup
1 and ½ cups chopped walnuts or pecans (May use
golden raisins or currants instead of nuts)

In a large mixing bowl combine dry cake mix, 2 cups of the flour, yeast, and salt. Add water and beat with an electric mixer on low speed until combined, scraping sides of bowl. Beat on high speed for 3 minutes. Stir in as much remaining flour as you can with a wooden spoon. Turn dough out onto a floured surface. Knead in enough of the remaining flour to make a smooth dough (about 3 minutes); dough will still be slightly sticky. Place dough in a large greased bowl. Cover and let rise in a warm place until doubled in size (about 1 hour). Punch dough down. Turn dough out onto a well-floured surface and divide in half. Cover and let stand for 10 minutes. Roll each portion out to form a 16 x 9 inch rectangle. Spread each rectangle with half of the quarter-cup butter. Sprinkle with mixture of granulated sugar and cinnamon. Starting from a long side, roll up dough into a log-spiral. Pinch to seal. Cut the dough into 1 inch slices.

In a saucepan, combine brown sugar, the 1 cup butter and corn syrup. Bring to boiling. Remove from heat. Divide mixture between two 13 x 9 x 2 inch baking pans. Sprinkle walnuts evenly into each pan. Place half of the rolls, cut side down, into each baking pan. Cover and refrigerate for 8 hours or overnight. When ready to bake, remove rolls from refrigerator and let stand at room temperature for 30 minutes.

Bake in a preheated 350 degree oven for about 25 minutes or until golden. Let cool for 10 minutes in pans on wire racks. Turn out onto foil. Serve warm or cooled. Cover and store at room temperature.

EASTER AND GREEK EASTER; BOTH CELEBRATE WITH LAMB

This is a very solemn holiday with fun traditions. Those who celebrate Greek Easter color eggs a scarlet red, usually on the prior Thursday evening. When baking begins these eggs are baked on top of a twisted sweet-bread loaf. Everyone loves to get one of the red eggs so there is usually a large bowl set aside holding extra.

If you are not celebrating Orthodox Easter, you will probably be coloring your eggs the night before Easter, usually all colors and decorations. These are then placed in a basket and left for the Easter bunny to hide.

Early Easter morning children look forward to hunting for the eggs, a favorite family time.

No matter which Easter you are observing, lamb will be roasting in many ovens, a tradition of Orthodox Easter, and a favorite entrée choice along with baked ham for non-Orthodox.

Enjoy this recipe at any time of the year which showcases roast lamb with a tasteful seasoning rub of rosemary and garlic.

ROAST LEG OF LAMB WITH A ROSEMARY GARLIC RUB

Prepare night before.

INGREDIENTS: *1 (5-6 pound) leg of lamb*
8 garlic cloves, peeled
3 tablespoons dried rosemary
1 and ½ tablespoons salt
1 and ½ teaspoons pepper
¾ cup olive oil

Remove as much fat and any skin from the lamb. With a sharp knife, cut 8 slits a few inches apart.

Cut 2 garlic cloves into 4 slices and insert a slice into each cut in the lamb. Mince remaining garlic and combine with rosemary, salt and pepper. Blend with ½ cup of the olive oil to make a thick, spreadable paste. Spread paste all over the lamb and rub in well. Cover and refrigerate overnight.

Before cooking, bring lamb to room temperature for an hour. Preheat oven to 375 degrees.
Roast lamb for 1 and ½ hours, or till meat thermometer reads 160 degrees (medium rare). Baste with remaining ¼ cup of olive oil 3 to 4 times during cooking.
Let lamb rest covered with aluminum foil for 10 minutes before carving; Serves 6 to 8.

May First Saturday; Kentucky Derby Festivities

You know what a "bucket list" refers to, i.e. a list of things you would like to do before you "kick the bucket."

Well, going to Kentucky Derby Week is tops on my list. I LOVE HATS!! And I could wear them there, big, flowery, gorgeous hats. I also wouldn't mind all the dressing up; after all, this is where high fashion meets Mardis Gras for one week of Balls and parties.

But the Kentucky Derby is more than that, it is the romantic old south wrapped around the most special horse race of the year. I tear up when they play "My Old Kentucky Home", and when the blanket of roses is placed atop the winner (hence nickname of the Derby, Run for the Roses). It is such an accomplishment for man and horse.

Derby cuisine has a draw all its own with traditions of the long-ago south and food classics like mint julep's, Hot Brown sandwiches, a vegetable stew called "burgoo", and heavenly chocolate-pecan pie served in almost every restaurant in Louisville.

So as I happily continue to enjoy this event at home, please join me in enjoying the following recipes. Spoon Bread is a specialty throughout the south, and beef tenderloin served with **Henry Bain Sauce** is exquisite. This zesty sauce was created in 1881 by Henry Bain, head waiter of a famous club in Louisville, Kentucky, and is enjoyed to this day, especially traditional during "Derby" week.

HENRY BAIN SAUCE (PRESENT DAY VERSION)

INGREDIENTS: *½ cup Major Grey's chutney; a thick, chunky, spicy condiment; (in market near steak sauce)*
1/3 cup bottled chili sauce
¼ cup Worcestershire sauce
2/3 cup ketchup
¼ cup steak sauce
¼ to ½ teaspoon hot sauce

Combine all, cover and refrigerate; does not need cooking or heating; serve at room temperature

ROAST BEEF TENDERLOIN

Rub a 2 ½ pound tenderloin with a mixture of 1 tablespoon olive oil, 1 tablespoon fresh snipped rosemary, 3 garlic cloves, minced, ¾ teaspoon salt, and ½ teaspoon pepper. Place on rack in a roaster, in pre-heated 425 degree oven, uncovered for 35-40 minutes for medium rare or 135 degrees on a meat thermometer. When done, cover with foil and let sit for 10 minutes before slicing.

SPOON BREAD (SOUFFLÉ-LIKE CORN BREAD)

INGREDIENTS: *¾ cup stone-ground yellow cornmeal*
1 teaspoon sugar
1 teaspoon salt
¼ teaspoon black pepper
2 ½ cups milk
¼ teaspoon hot sauce (optional)
2 large egg yolks
1 tablespoon soft butter
½ teaspoon baking powder
3 large egg whites

Preheat oven to 350 degrees. Coat an 11"x 7" baking dish with cooking spray.

Combine cornmeal, sugar, salt, and pepper in a large saucepan; stir in milk and hot sauce. Cook over medium heat until thick, about 15 minutes, stirring constantly. Place egg yolks in a medium bowl. Spoon ½ cup hot cornmeal mixture into egg yolks, then stir entire yolk mixture into remaining cornmeal mixture. Add butter, stirring until it melts.

Place baking powder and egg whites in a medium bowl; beat with mixer at high speed until stiff peaks form. Using a spatula, {gently fold a third of egg white mixture at a time into cornmeal mixture; be patient as this is a slow step}, it's ok to see a few pieces of the egg whites. Spoon mixture into baking dish; bake for 40 minutes or until lightly browned and puffy; especially good with barbecued cuisine.

Mother's Day

Who doesn't like being queen for a day? When my sons were teens they decided to prepare dinner for me, which included food shopping and clean-up. They decided the menu, as I preferred being surprised, and was further surprised when I saw candles and a tablecloth. At their insistence I was to take a leisurely walk, and then pick a good movie on television, or get into a good book and do nothing.

My favorite memory was listening to the laughing and camaraderie of my boys as they went about the preparation. They had no idea that they were giving me everlasting memories that I treasure. Their working together, laughing together, and enjoying each other was truly the best part of my special day.

Today, if someone were to cook for me for Mother's Day, I would request Shrimp and Pea Risotto. I first enjoyed this dish when my cousin Paul, a foodie such as myself, made it when I visited him, his wife Carol, and my aunt and uncle in Connecticut. I have always been grateful to Paul for teaching me how to make a good Risotto, intimidating to me in the past; I found it to be quite easy. Continuous stirring is the secret. Just enjoy good company and a glass of wine while you are stirring.

Shrimp and Pea Risotto

INGREDIENTS: *2 tablespoons olive oil*
1 medium onion, chopped/minced
2 cups Arborio rice, No substitutions
1 cup white wine (chardonnay or sauvignon Blanc is suggested)
Generous pinch saffron threads (ok to omit or substitute ¼ teaspoon turmeric).

3 (14.5 ounce) cans chicken broth (heat chicken broth
short of boiling, than keep on simmer).
Salt and fresh ground black pepper to taste
4 tablespoons grated parmesan cheese
2 tablespoons butter
2 pounds large shrimp, cleaned and deveined (ok to use
pre-cooked)
1 bag frozen baby peas

Cooking process is all done at medium heat or slightly less. Heat chicken broth in a separate pan. In a large saucepan, soften onions in 2 tablespoons olive oil, about 3 minutes. Add rice and stir to coat the grains. Let cook about 3 minutes, stirring frequently. Stir in wine and saffron. The process of adding the chicken stock will be a ladle at a time, ½ cup, (just till rice is covered), all the while stirring while it gets creamy, and is absorbed. This will take about 20 minutes. Keep adding broth slowly. The bottom of the pan should be clean. Add salt and pepper to taste. Add shrimp and peas, cook 5to 8 minutes till hot. Add butter and parmesan cheese, stir to mix in. Makes 4 to 6 servings.

In the 1950's, my mother was all about cakes and pies. My choice for this present Mothers' Day would be cake. And this cake is special. In 1959 Eunice Surles of Louisiana, became the first southern woman to win the Pillsbury Bake-Off. She won the grand prize with this **Mardi Gras Party Cake**, a heavenly concoction of butterscotch, coconut, and "sea foam" frosting. I'm sure she would be honored that it is still being made today.

Mardi Gras Party Cake

CAKE INGREDIENTS: *2/3 cup butterscotch chips*
¼ cup water
2 ¼ cups all-purpose flour

1 ¼ cups sugar
1 teaspoon baking soda
1 teaspoon salt
½ teaspoon baking powder
1 cup buttermilk
½ cup shortening (such as Crisco brand)
3 eggs

FILLING: *½ cup sugar*
1 tablespoon cornstarch
½ cup half-and-half or evaporated milk
1/3 cup water
1/3 cup butterscotch chips
1 egg, slightly beaten
2 tablespoons butter
1 cup coconut
1 cup chopped nuts
Seafoam cream frosting:
1cup whipping cream
¼ cup firmly packed brown sugar
½ teaspoon vanilla

1. Heat oven to 350 degrees. Generously grease and flour two 9-inch round cake pans. In small saucepan over low heat, melt 2/3 cup butterscotch chips in ¼ cup water, stirring until smooth. Cool slightly.
2. Lightly spoon flour into measuring cup; level off. In large bowl, combine flour, all remaining cake ingredients and cooled butterscotch mixture; beat at low speed until moistened. Beat 3 minutes at medium speed. Pour batter into greased and floured pans. Bake for 20 to 30 minutes or until toothpick inserted in center comes out clean. Cool 10 minutes; remove from pans. Cool 30 minutes or until completely cooled.

3. In medium saucepan, combine half cup sugar and cornstarch; stir in half-and-half, a third cup water, a third cup butterscotch chips and 1 egg. Cook over medium heat until mixture thickens, stirring constantly. Remove from heat. Stir in butter, coconut and nuts; cool slightly. 4. In small bowl, beat whipping cream until soft peaks form. Gradually add brown sugar and vanilla, beating until stiff peaks form. 6. To assemble cake, place 1 cake layer, top side down, on serving plate. Spread with half of filling mixture. Top with second layer, top side up; spread remaining filling on top to within 1/2 inch of edge; Frost sides and **top edges** of cake with seafoam frosting. Refrigerate at least 1 hour before serving; Store in refrigerator.

If I were cooking for my mother, I would plan to have a Family Brunch in her honor, where everyone could participate and bring a favorite dish. I would make this delectable **French Toast Croissant**, which she would love enjoying with Mimosa's and her family!

FRENCH TOAST, CROISSANT STYLE

INGREDIENTS: *Vanilla sauce:*

1 tablespoon all-purpose flour

4 egg yolks

1 tablespoon vanilla extract

2 cups whipping cream

1/2 cup sugar

2 scoops vanilla ice cream

BERRY SAUCE: *Combine 2 cups unsweetened strawberries with 2 tablespoons sugar.*

French toast:

4 croissants split

3 eggs

2 tablespoons butter

In a bowl, combine flour, egg yolks and vanilla; set aside.

In a saucepan over medium heat, bring the whipping cream and sugar to a boil; remove from the heat. Stir in a small amount of the hot cream into egg yolk mixture; return all to the pan, stirring constantly. Bring to a gentle boil; cook and stir for 2 minutes. Remove from the heat; stir in ice cream until melted. Set aside.

For the berry sauce, combine strawberries and sugar in a saucepan. (May substitute raspberries) Simmer uncovered for 2-3 minutes. Remove from heat and set aside.

To prepare croissants: In a shallow bowl, beat eggs. Dip both sides of croissants in egg mixture. On a griddle, brown croissants on both sides in butter. Serve with vanilla and berry sauces, Makes 4 servings.

Memorial Day Weekend over the Years

It always signified the beginning of the summer season, but every few years our destination changed. When my children were babies and toddlers, we headed up to the White Mountains of New Hampshire with camper in tow. We were ready for all that goes with camping; cooking out, visiting and playing cards with friends, and making the rounds of day excursions to children's attractions such as the Polar Caves (my boys will never forget the rock formation called Lemon Squeeze) and Santa's Village. Those years went by fast, and in their early school years, we spent Memorial Day at home enjoying Little League games, supporting our sons on their first athletic teams. Many of those weekend evenings were spent on the esplanade in Lowell Massachusetts at an evening outdoor concert, enjoying a blanket picnic and watching boat races before it got dark.

As my boys are men now, I enjoy going back to my own hometown of Southboro, Massachusetts to watch the parade and ceremonies that are led by our Veterans, my brother and friends among them. I am always humbled by their speeches, camaraderie and commitment.

What does not change over the years are the "main ingredients" of any holiday weekend; family, friends, fun, and good food. I always made something red, white, and blue, like the **Red, White & Blue Fruit Pizza**, which consists of colorful fruit and a layer of sweetened cream cheese on a pecan-shortbread cookie crust, made on a pizza pan.

The **Cashew Chicken Salad** was always popular as is, yet can be dressed up by serving on a croissant with a garnish of green grapes. And the **Brownie Shortcake** is so quick and so good I had to include it.

RED, WHITE, AND BLUE FRUIT PIZZA

CRUST INGREDIENTS:
1 cup all-purpose flour
¼ cup confectioners' sugar
½ cup cold butter, cut into pieces
½ cup finely chopped pecans

CREAM CHEESE LAYER: *1 package (8 ounces) cream cheese, 1 egg, and 1/3 cup sugar*

FRUIT SPREAD:
1 bag frozen mixed berries, thawed (1 ¾ cups)
½ cup sugar
2 tablespoons cornstarch
¼ cup water

TOPPINGS: *Approximately 4 cups of fresh sliced strawberries and 2 cups of blueberries*

1 container of whipped topping; about 2 cups
thawed

GLAZE: *½ cup strawberry jelly, melted*

Make crust: Preheat oven to 350 degrees. In a bowl, combine flour and confectioners' sugar. Cut in cold butter until crumbly. Stir in pecans. Press firmly onto an ungreased 12 inch pizza pan. Bake for 12 to 14 minutes until crust is set and edges are golden brown.

Cream cheese layer: While crust is baking, beat cream cheese, egg, and sugar until smooth. Spread over the HOT crust and return to oven to bake another 8-10 minutes longer or until set. Cool to room temperature.

Fruit spread: In a blender, mix thawed berries and sugar until blended. In a medium saucepan, combine cornstarch and water until smooth. Add the pureed berry mixture. Bring to a boil; cook and stir for 2 minutes or until thickened. Set saucepan in ice water for 15 minutes, stirring several times. Spread this mixture over the room temperature cream cheese layer.

To form the red, white, and blue arrangement, spread the whipped topping around the outer edge of the pizza, not too thick, about 2 inches wide. Arrange sliced strawberries close to the whipped topping. Continue in a circle with the blueberries. If I have more strawberries, I add them now, and finish with a large dollop of whipped topping in the very center. Lightly brush the fresh berries with the melted jelly. This gives them a shiny glaze finish, and keeps the fruit from looking dried out. Refrigerate at least 2 hours before slicing into wedges.

Cashew Chicken Salad

INGREDIENTS: *4 cups cut-up cooked chicken*
1 cup finely chopped celery
½ cup chopped green pepper
1 (2 ounce) jar diced pimentos, drained
½ cup mayonnaise
1/3 cup whipping cream
¼ cup sour cream
3 tablespoons thinly sliced green onions
2 tablespoons minced fresh parsley
1 ½ teaspoons of each; lemon juice and cider vinegar
1 garlic clove, minced
½ teaspoon of each; salt & pepper
¾ cup salted cashews

In a large bowl, combine chicken, celery, green pepper and pimentos; set aside. In a blender, combine remaining ingredients except garlic, salt & pepper, and cashews, blending until well mixed. Add garlic, salt, and pepper to chicken mixture and toss lightly. Pour blender ingredients over chicken and toss. Cover and refrigerate. When ready to serve fold in the cashews. Serve in a lettuce-lined serving bowl, or spoon onto open-sliced croissants.

Garnish with chopped cashews and grapes. Makes about 6 servings.

Brownie Shortcake with Sour Cream Topping

Preheat oven to 350 degrees

INGREDIENTS: *1 box (19.5 ounce) brownie mix*
1 container (16 ounces) sour cream, divided
1 cup thawed whipped topping

1 tablespoon confectioners' sugar
1 teaspoon vanilla
Fresh sliced strawberries and blueberries, combined to
  make 3 cups

Prepare brownie batter as directed on package; stir in ½ cup of the sour cream; spoon into a greased and floured 9 inch round cake pan. Bake 45 minutes; cool 10 minutes. Remove from pan to wire rack; cool completely. Mix remaining sour cream, whipped topping, sugar and vanilla. Cut brownie in half horizontally to make 2 layers. Place bottom half on a serving plate; spread with half of the sour cream mixture. Cover with top of brownie and remaining sour cream mixture. Pile berries in center of top to complete red, white, blue theme; Store in refrigerator.

Comment from Lois, Methuen   *I just had to tell you about your Brownie Shortcake that I made this past weekend for dessert at a barbecue we went to. HIT OF THE EVENING! No exaggeration. Where did you get such a great recipe is what I want to know? Many recipes say how easy they are, but you were right about this one, really easy. I plan to make it again for July 4ᵗʰ and use raspberries on top.*

June: Father's Day — Honoring the Many Fathers in My Life

My grandfather raised his six sons on Hazelcroft Farm in Hopkinton Massachusetts in the 1930s. His life was physical work from daybreak to sunset.

Even in the winter, his skin would be brown from the sun. He was such an easy going man, and I never heard him raise his voice. He was always there when we needed him. With excerpts from a poem I once read, I can describe him in these ways that I remember him the most: "A man with the warmth of the summer sun, the calm of a peaceful lake, and the wisdom of the ages;" If you had only known him.

My father raised his family from mid 1940's into the 1970's. He was a hardworking man who often worked three jobs to "put a roof over our heads, keep us warm and fed well", all important necessities to the bread-winner of those years. Christmas morning seemed to be his favorite time of year. His eyes were brighter, his brow less worrisome, his smile bigger as he watched his eight children open their gifts. It took me many years to appreciate what an accomplishment that was at the time, to give that many kids a good Christmas.

Since the early 2000s I have watched the newest Dads in my family, my nephews, raise their young children. Chris, Steve, Ed, Todd, Dave, James, Dan, and Paul inspire me. They not only work many hours at their jobs, but they are active partners in parenting. They do diapering and "walking the floors" to soothe their crying baby and they go to all school and sports events. I see them parent with encouragement, support, and lots of affection, play and fun. Being a Mother, I never paid a lot of attention to Father's Day, but these young fathers deserve the honor of their day, they continue to earn it, and they have my respect.

All the guys would go for these pulled pork sliders that "Papa Mike" made for Brianna's High School graduation party.

MIKE'S PULLED PORK SLIDERS;
COURTESY MIKE OF CONWAY NH

INGREDIENTS: *1 Boston pork butt, 4 ½ to 5 pounds*
2 sweet onions, such as Vidalia
1 (12 ounce) can ginger ale

> *1 (18 ounce) bottle Sweet Baby Rays barbecue sauce*
> *(more is optional)*

In a large slow cooker, place 2 halves of one onion on bottom. Place pork butt on top of onion. Place the remaining onion, also cut in half, on top of pork. Pour in ginger ale. Cook on low for 12 hours. DO NOT OPEN the slow cooker. Next, drain off the liquid. Shred pork meat and onions when cool enough to handle (shred with forks or your fingers). Return shredded pork to crock-pot, add barbecue sauce, adjusting amount to your taste. Cook on low an additional 2 hours. Serve on "sliders" rolls, top with coleslaw; Makes 8 servings.

This coleslaw recipe is perfect for pulled pork sandwiches as it is mildly flavored and does not overpower the pork;

What it does do is give you a cool, crisp layer of texture, which complements the meat.

Mike's Coleslaw; Courtesy Mike of Conway NH

INGREDIENTS: *1 medium head green cabbage, finely shredded*
1 ¼ cup mayonnaise
5 tablespoons apple cider vinegar
¼ cup sugar or equivalent sugar substitute

Mix all ingredients together, refrigerate overnight; drain off any liquid as you build the slider.

MY DAD'S RHUBARB HAD ROOTS

Since Fathers' Day falls in June, my father would request one of his favorites, rhubarb pie. From April to June he would enjoy rhubarb fixed as many ways as my mother could think of. Cakes, cobbler, and pies were abundant. According to my grandfather, raising our own rhubarb goes back at least five generations. When my grandparents downsized from Hazelcroft farm to a smaller home, he transplanted his rhubarb to the new house. When my grandfather died and that house sold, my father transplanted the same rhubarb to his garden. Dad again took those rhubarb plants to Cape Cod when he retired, and I transplanted two of the same plants to my garden after he died. Our rhubarb certainly has "roots".

For Dad, Rhubarb Pie

Dish a Wedding gift in 1905 to Author's Grandparents.

INGREDIENTS: *4 cups finely cut rhubarb*
2 ½ tablespoons minute tapioca
1- 1/3 cup sugar
¼ teaspoon salt
Scant 1 tablespoon butter

Mix together rhubarb, tapioca, sugar and salt, let sit for 10 minutes then pour into a 9 inch pie crust. Drop butter pieces over rhubarb. Cover with top crust; crimp edges. Bake in a 425 pre-heated oven (on lowest rack) for 10 minutes. Lower heat to 350 degrees and bake about 40 minutes more until crust is lightly browned.

Note: Strawberries can be used to replace half of the rhubarb.

Pie crust: Use pre-made pastry for 9 inch double crust pie, or my mother's recipe below:

STELLA JACKMAN'S NEVER FAIL PIE CRUST

Makes (2) 9 inch double crusts

INGREDIENTS: *4 cups flour*
1 tablespoon sugar
2 teaspoons salt
1 ¾ cup shortening (may use half butter or butter-flavored shortening)
1 egg, beaten
Scant 2/3 cup cold water
1 tablespoon white vinegar

Mix flour, sugar, and salt. Add shortening with pastry blender and mix well. Mix egg, vinegar, and water; add to flour mixture mixing with fork then hands till well blended. Separate into 4 discs, refrigerate tightly wrapped until ready to use or immediately roll out to about 1/8th inch thick.

(Will keep up to 2 weeks refrigerated, or freeze up to 2 months.)

Note: There are many versions of "never fail" pie crust; this was my mother's recipe since the early 1980's.

July 4th: Independence Day

There is something magical about fireworks on the Fourth of July. I have enjoyed them from a boat in Boston harbor, a hill-top in Wolfeboro New Hampshire, Chatham pier, Cape Cod, and my own hometown.

My brother Bill says the best fireworks are in the city of Buenos Aires when it seems the entire city is magnificently lit.

Grilled Turkey Breast

A plus to this recipe is that the marinade has no sugar and is low fat, while very delicious.

INGREDIENTS: *1 turkey breast half with bone in (2-2 ½ pounds will feed 4-6 people)*
1 cup plain yogurt
¼ cup lemon juice
3 tablespoons olive oil
¼ cup minced fresh parsley
¼ cup chopped green onions
2 garlic cloves, minced
2 tablespoons minced fresh dill, or 2 teaspoons dried dill weed
½ teaspoon crushed dried rosemary
½ teaspoon salt and ¼ teaspoon pepper

Place turkey breast in a glass baking dish. In a small bowl, combine remaining ingredients. Spread over the turkey. Cover tightly and refrigerate at least 8 hours or overnight. Turn to coat a couple of times. Remove turkey and discard marinade. Grill turkey covered, over medium heat (charcoal or gas grill), for 1 to 1¼ hours or till juices run clear. It is better to go lower on the heat and cook longer to keep it moist. Turn turkey a few times during cooking.

PRETTY POPPY STRAWBERRY PIE

INGREDIENTS: *Pastry: 1and 1/3 cup all-purpose flour*
1 tablespoon poppy seeds
¼ teaspoon salt
½ cup shortening, cold
3 tablespoons ice water
Filling: 2 pints strawberries, divided
1 tablespoon powdered sugar
¼ teaspoon almond extract or orange extract
2 cups whipped topping or whipped cream
2 tablespoons honey OR melted strawberry jelly
¼ cup slivered almonds, lightly toasted (optional)

In a bowl combine flour, poppy seeds and salt; cut in cold shortening until crumbly. Gradually add water, tossing with a fork until dough forms a ball. Roll out pastry to fit **9 inch** pie plate; line plate with pastry, flute edges. Line unpricked pastry with a double thickness of heavy-duty foil. Bake at 450 degrees for 8 minutes. Remove foil; bake 5 minutes longer. Cool thoroughly.

Slice 1 pint strawberries and add 1 tablespoon powdered sugar and ¼ teaspoon orange extract; fold into whipped cream or whipped topping, spoon into pie shell. Cut remaining berries in half, arrange on top. Drizzle with honey or glaze strawberries with melted jelly; Sprinkle with toasted almonds. Refrigerate for 1 hour before serving.

SEPTEMBER: LABOR DAY — NATIONAL HOLIDAY SINCE 1894

How It All Began......Peter McGuire started it all! One of ten children living in New York City, Peter had to go to work at eleven years old. He did factory work, twelve-hour days for years. When older he fought for and won eight hour work days for workers. He became president of the Brotherhood of Carpenters and argued that a special honor be given to the industrial men and spirit of the country, as a vital force of the nation. In September 1882, New York held the first Labor Day event. A parade of 10,000 people marched carrying signs saying the following: "All Men are Born Equal". Twelve years later it became a National holiday.

AN OLD FASHIONED PICNIC

What can be better than an old fashioned picnic on Labor Day?

A huge family picnic on blankets in the backyard or in a Park, picnic baskets and coolers nearby, chairs if needed, lots of kids with Frisbees, music, and always a horseshoe game set up by the men. Memorable!

Many in my family head for the White Mountains of New Hampshire for Labor Day weekend, enjoying a picnic on the banks of the Saco River while watching a continuous stream of kayaks and canoes pass by.

On my "wish list", enjoying a Labor Day picnic in Central Park, New York while listening to a great outdoor concert.

Tips:

1. Pack as many foods as possible in cardboard containers like ones Chinese food comes in. You can find these in most party stores, and they are better than plastic containers. You can just throw them in the trash.

2. A disposable tablecloth, be festive (in party stores).

3. Bag cookies, brownies, pieces watermelon, etc. in individual baggies.

4. For a "Quick Picnic", such as on a date, bring a picnic basket to your local deli and stuff with deli foods.

What is a picnic without WATERMELON? Here is a way to bring that watermelon flavor up a notch: Cut watermelon into serving pieces and pack into a large plastic container. Liberally squeeze on the juice of several limes. I use 6 limes for half a watermelon. Cover and keep refrigerated or in a cooler.

BUTTERMILK FRIED CHICKEN

INGREDIENTS: *10 to 12 pieces of chicken cut into serving size if large*
3 cups buttermilk or enough to cover chicken
1/3 to ½ cup hot sauce (for bold & spicy); Optional, or decrease amount for mild
2 cups flour
1 tablespoon salt
1 tablespoon dry mustard
3 teaspoons ground cayenne (for bold & spicy) – Optional, or decrease to 1 teaspoon for mild heat.
2 teaspoons fresh ground black pepper

Combine buttermilk with hot sauce (if using, adjust to taste, mild to bold), pour mixture over chicken to cover; let marinate for 3 hours or overnight. Combine flour and remaining seasonings in a paper bag. After marinating, let chicken drain on racks for a few minutes. Shake a few pieces of chicken at a time in the flour, shake off excess and place on waxed paper next to stove. In a large skillet, heat about a half inch of cooking oil to medium hot (takes about 8 minutes to get hot enough, few drops of water sprinkled in should sizzle). Hint: Getting oil properly hot is what keeps oil from soaking into chicken. Fry chicken skin-side down first, about 12 minutes on first side, turn and fry about 10 minutes on other side. Use a splatter screen if you have one. Do not put a cover on. When golden brown, take chicken out and drain on wire rack or brown paper.

If bringing to an outdoor picnic, purchase a cardboard bucket at hardware or party store, keeps chicken at its crispiest.

TEXAS CAVIAR

There are many versions of this "Dip & Eat" snack, and this is my favorite. The first time I made it I quadrupled the recipe, and it was quickly gone. A winner with the guys and football games!

INGREDIENTS: *1 cup olive oil*
½ cup sugar
1 cup apple cider vinegar
1(16 ounce) can black beans, drained and rinsed
1 (16 ounce) can black eyed peas – drained and rinsed
1 (12 ounce) can whole kernel corn – drained and rinsed
1 medium red onion, chopped fine
3 tablespoons jalapeno rings, chopped fine (found in pickle section)

Combine all ingredients and soak overnight. Before serving, strain off oil and vinegar; serve with "scoops" dipping crackers.

WHOOPIE PIES; AKA DEVIL DOGS

Wrapped individually these are easy to handle at a picnic.

My Aunt Jane used this recipe for many years, in fact when she sent me the recipe it is a copy of the original newspaper clipped from the Boston Daily Globe, circa 1950's.

My brother Bill never told our Mother that Aunt Jane's whoopee pies were his favorite over her recipe, although he ate any that were given to him. Long after our Mom died, he asked me if I could get Jane's recipe and make them. I did, and he was right; these stay moist and the filling is delicious.

INGREDIENTS: *½ cup shortening (such as Crisco brand)*
1 ½ cups sugar
2 eggs, beaten
1 teaspoon vanilla extract
2 and ¾ cups all-purpose flour, sifted
½ teaspoon salt
1 teaspoon baking soda
½ cup cocoa
½ cup sour milk or buttermilk

Cream shortening and sugar; add eggs and vanilla. Sift flour, salt, soda, and cocoa; add buttermilk and mix well. This is a very stiff batter and I mix by hand if necessary. Drop from tablespoon and flatten with a glass dipped in flour, or force through a cookie press using the lady-finger tip.

Bake at 350 degrees about 10 minutes. Put together sandwich fashion with the following filling.

Filling: Cook to thick paste, and then cool until very thick: 1 ½ tablespoons flour, 1 tablespoon cornstarch, and ½ cup milk. Then add ½ cup shortening, ½ cup sugar, and 1 teaspoon vanilla. Beat with electric mixer until very light and fluffy. Makes about 24 individual cookies, or 12 whoopie pies.

Note: Even making a single batch, I would double the filling amounts.

Rosh Hashanah: Symbolic Food Facts

September brings this holiday of reflection and self-evaluation. Some interesting food facts are that fish is very often served, along with apples, honey, pomegranates, and beets. Apples and honey are commonly used together, meaning "may we be sent a sweet and fruitful year". Serving pomegranates wishes "the coming year be rich with blessings as this fruit is rich with seeds". Enjoy the recipes included here that highlight these symbolic beliefs.

Honey-Raisin Baked Apples

Preheat oven to 350 degrees

INGREDIENTS: *4 medium-large tart apples, cored (careful to not cut through bottom)*
½ cup raisins
2 tablespoons honey
½ teaspoon apple pie spice (ok plain cinnamon)
½ teaspoon grated lemon rind/zest
¼ cup chopped pecans (optional)
½ cup apple juice

Peel a wide strip from around the top-third of each apple (an old-time technique which keeps skins from splitting during baking).

Place apples in a 9 inch baking pan or pie pan.

In a small bowl, combine raisins, honey, apple pie spice, lemon rind, apple juice and nuts if using. Spoon this mixture into the center of apples. Pour any leftover juice into the pan.

Bake 40-45 minutes until apples are just tender, basting occasionally using pan juices.

APPLE-HONEY CAKE

Very pretty baked in a Bundt pan and simply dusted with confectioners' sugar. Anyone will enjoy this.

Preheat oven to 325 degrees

INGREDIENTS: *2 eggs*
1 cup vegetable oil
1 ¼ cups sugar
¾ cup honey
1 teaspoon vanilla
4 cups peeled and thinly sliced apples (you don't want big chunks for this cake)
2 ½ cups all-purpose flour
1 teaspoon <u>each</u>: baking soda, baking powder, and salt
½ teaspoon ground cloves and 1 teaspoon ground cinnamon
¾ cup chopped walnuts

Beat eggs and oil in a mixing bowl until foamy. Add sugar, honey (slowly, continuing to mix), and vanilla. Beat well. Combine flour, baking soda, baking powder, salt, cinnamon, and cloves (do this with a wire whisk). Add to egg mixture gradually and beat continuously until all mixed well. Stir in apples and walnuts. Pour into a Bundt pan that has been greased and floured well. Bake for 50-60 minutes until cake tests done (toothpick comes out dry). Let cool 15 minutes before turning out onto cake plate. When totally cooled, sprinkle with confectioner's sugar.

Comments from Helen D. *I made the Apple Cake with honey a few months ago and it was fantastic. I saved the recipe but can't find it. I'm a sucker for cooking and made several of your recipes, all wonderful. I'm going broke feeding my friends. With the s.a.s.e. please send the recipe.*

Comment from Sue R. *I made your Apple-Honey Cake this morning. It is delicious.*

OCTOBER: HALLOWEEN — ENJOYING AS MUCH AS THE KIDS

I loved the fun of it all, from having a houseful of children for a spooky party, coming up with that year's costumes, to cutting out the candle-lit pumpkin that sat on our front steps at sunset and welcomed all the trick-or-treaters. Our spooky parties were the best when the kids were in the third to sixth grades. Usually fifteen to twenty school friends were invited, and the parties were held in our basement. The favorite part was being blindfolded and going through the "corner of horror", where a sheet blocked off a table where fingers could be jabbed into "eyeballs" (bowl of olives), "guts" (cold strands of spaghetti), "a heart" (raw liver), and much more. One year I won the prize for the scariest party because the girls said they screamed the loudest and were totally scared. Of course the ghoulish music helped. All the kids never had a clue that I enjoyed it as much as they did. I loved fixing up "black spider cupcakes", beef stew baked in a pumpkin shell, and for breakfast, what else but pumpkin pancakes. I searched magazines for awesome and different ideas and here are some good ones.

The boys love making this first one, and the girls love being "grossed out".

Cozy, Critter-Filled Pumpkin:

First, pick out a large uncarved pumpkin. Next, use a black marker to draw circles for several small holes, about ten or twelve. Have an adult cut out the holes; no scraping inside the pumpkin is needed. Fill the holes with rubber mice (found at party stores) peeking out, and some with the tails sticking out.

Create A Spooky Table:

For the centerpiece, purchase a cut-out pumpkin with a light in it, or use a battery-operated candle set inside. Place this in center of table and throw a white sheet over it, gathering and tying at the pumpkin base. Cover the base with a string of decorations (keep in mind dollar stores). Spread the sheet out over the table. Simply scatter on the sheet items such as candy corn, webbing, plastic spiders, and other creepy things you can find. Top the pumpkin with a black hat. When the room is darkened and the pumpkin lit, it will look very spooky, and eating meals there will be a special treat.

Favorite Goodies: Jiggle Pumpkins

This spooky snack is a finger-food that toddlers especially love; they are as cute as can be and easy enough to make. If you do not have a pumpkin-shaped cookie cutter, use any round cutter. Makes about 14 individual treats.

INGREDIENTS: *2 packages (6 ounces each) orange jello*
2 ½ cups boiling water
1 cup cold whole milk
1 package (3.4 ounce) instant vanilla pudding mix
candy corn for eyes and black licorice or black gumdrops
for candy mouths

Dissolve gelatin in water; set aside for 30 minutes. Whisk milk and pudding mix until smooth, about 1 minute.

Quickly pour into gelatin; whisk until well blended. Pour into an oiled 13"x9"x2" pan. Chill until set. Cut into circles or use pumpkin cookie cutter, place on serving plate. Just before serving decorate with candy eyes and mouths.

Pumpkin Pancakes

Since Halloween often comes on a school night, I suggest prepping the night before by having dry ingredients measured in a mixing bowl. Pre-measure canned pumpkin, and have oil, chocolate chips, and griddle out and ready.

INGREDIENTS: *1 cup all-purpose flour*
1 cup quick cooking oats
2 tablespoons wheat germ
2 teaspoons sugar
2 teaspoons baking powder
½ teaspoon salt
pinch of ground cinnamon or pumpkin pie spice

1 cup whole milk
1 egg, lightly beaten
¾ cup canned pumpkin
2 tablespoons vegetable oil
Chocolate chips or raisins for decorating

In a bowl, combine flour, oats, wheat germ, sugar, baking powder, salt, and cinnamon. Combine milk, egg, pumpkin and oil; stir into dry ingredients just until moistened. Pour batter by ¼ cupfuls onto a hot greased griddle; turn when bubbles form on top of pancakes. Cook until second side is golden brown. Serve with butter and cinnamon-sugar mix or syrup. Using chocolate chips or raisins make smiley faces; Makes about 10 pancakes.

COOL, DESSERT IS IN THE PUMPKIN!

In 1997, I was managing a Home Health office in Haverhill. We had several visiting nurses on our staff. One of the nurses had made a visit to a gentleman who lived alone, and was nearing ninety years old. She said she entered the house, and the aroma of spice and cinnamon welcomed her. On the counter was a pumpkin, heaped high with bread pudding that had just come out of the oven. Since this gentleman had lost his wife, and was confined to home for medical reasons, he explained his love for cooking, the enjoyment coming from choosing different recipes from his wife's collection. After the nurse finished her visit exam and paperwork, he showed her to the table, where he had a heaping bowl of warm bread pudding covered with some heavy cream, waiting for her.

When she returned to the office, she told me of her visit and said the most difficult part of caring for this client would be for her not to gain weight. Over time though, he did most of his cooking for his devoted neighbors who watched out for him. I asked Paula to see if she could get me the recipe and she did. I still have it, in his handwriting, and have made it several times over the years.

Young children like it on Halloween because it is warm and tastes good. With the eggs, milk, and raisins, it is also something nutritious for them to eat before all the trick or treat candy, and they think it is cool that it comes out of a pumpkin.

Bread Pudding Baked in Pumpkin Shell

Preheat oven to 350 degrees

INGREDIENTS: *1/3 cup sugar*
2 cups milk
¼ cup butter
3 cups stale bread cubes (ciabatta loaf, French bread stick) use hearty bread
3 eggs
½ to 2/3 cup raisins; amount to your personal taste
¼ teaspoon salt
1 teaspoon cinnamon
½ teaspoon nutmeg
1 teaspoon vanilla extract
1/2 cup chopped pecans - optional

Hollow out a medium-sized pumpkin, removing seeds and stringy pulp. Wipe off outside shell.

Combine milk and butter in a medium saucepan; cook over medium heat until butter melts. Add sugar and stir until sugar dissolves, remove from heat. Combine bread cubes, raisins and pecans in a large bowl;

toss gently. Pour milk mixture over bread mixture and stir gently. In a small bowl, beat eggs with vanilla, nutmeg, salt, and cinnamon; add to bread mix and stir gently. Spoon mixture into pumpkin; place in middle of oven, on oven rack lined with aluminum foil. Bake uncovered for about 1 hour or until pudding lightly browns, is set, and knife inserted in center comes out clean. Serve warm. Makes 6-8 servings

A Thanksgiving Wish for You,

May your spirit be uplifted
by the cool, crisp autumn air.
May your heart be filled with
special moments to share
and treasures to be found
as you celebrate Thanksgiving.

Treasure Family Traditions

Our family Thanksgiving dinner has always been rich in tradition, and every year I find it still inspires and awes me.

My parents came from large families and had eight children themselves, so from the 1950s on, the table was filled and a second table was added for many years (the famous kids' table). I hold many memories in my heart but one that stands out is the pie table that began with my grandmother in the 1920s and 30s, when my father said there would be at least two to three pies of each kind, and there were six different kinds; apple, pumpkin, squash, mock cherry, mincemeat, and an occasional custard or blueberry. My mother continued the tradition, adding her favorite of pecan pie.

Also, what stuffing you serve on Thanksgiving can get quite personal. My mother treasured her basic sage bread stuffing with turkey giblets, onions and celery. Several family members (including my father and several uncles) favor my paternal grandmother's oyster stuffing, quahogs substituted by my mother when oysters were too costly. Many Thanksgivings both kinds were served.

Thanksgiving is a lot of work, and one of my favorite memories is my father becoming my mom's self-appointed assistant over the years. He would search out the best sugar pumpkins from local farm stands for pies, then cut and peel them for her as she pureed the pumpkin for fresh pumpkin pie. On Thanksgiving eve, he would join her in the kitchen after supper, to peel and prep all the vegetables while she made pies, both quietly working together.

CANDIED SWEET POTATOES

I have absolutely no idea where or how this dish originated in my family, but it has been on our Thanksgiving and Christmas table since we were small children. I do know it was a favorite of my mother. I also know she never had a written recipe and always cooked them in an electric skillet as there was no room in the oven or on top of the stove.

My sister-in-law Donna, niece Keri and nephew Todd are carrying on the tradition in their homes with their families, and Donnas' candied "sweets" are as delicious as my Mother's.

I have made them many times; potatoes in the pan, keep adding butter and brown sugar till thick and syrupy, cooking slow, basting often and turning.

Below is the basic recipe to start with. Just remember it is ok to add more brown sugar until it is thick and syrupy.

Also if you do not have an electric fry pan, use a covered skillet on the stove, cooking slowly.

INGREDIENTS: *6 medium-size sweet potatoes, approximately 3 pounds, peeled and cut into thick slices (1 ½ to 2 inch)*
1 teaspoon salt and ½ teaspoon fresh ground black pepper
2 sticks butter (1 cup)
1 cup dark brown sugar, packed

Melt butter in pan; add potatoes, salt and pepper. Sprinkle on brown sugar and stir to coat. Cook on medium low, stirring several times, until potatoes done and coated with thick syrup. The longer they cook, the more caramelized they become. These are even better the next day when reheated. Yield 6-8 servings.

MY MOTHER'S FAVORITE, BAKED INDIAN PUDDING

And the very best recipe for it can be found in a Boston Massachusetts restaurant where it has been made the same way for 150 years plus; **Durgin-Park,** a century-old restaurant in Faneuil Hall Market Place, going back to 1742 when the fame of its Indian Pudding, chowders, baked beans, and other famous dishes developed over time. What a fascinating place; it can be noisy with dishes clanging and boxes and crates piled in a corner, but that doesn't stop people from all over the world to come in for thick slabs of rare roast beef, bear steak in the winter, and huge bowls of New England boiled dinners set in the center of a long table that seats twenty people, no fancy dining here, just good food and fascinating history. I quote an excerpt from their story-telling brochure:

"Every morning at 11, for the past 42 years, a retired sea captain has dined on chowder, Indian pudding and coffee. Twice a week, for the past 44 years, a little old lady from Beacon Hill comes in at 5 pm and orders two man-size portions of Indian pudding and nothing else."

Some history about this Classic New England dessert, Indian pudding, says that early Colonists brought with them to America a fondness for British "hasty pudding", a dish made by boiling wheat flour in water or milk until it thickened into porridge. Since wheat flour was scarce in the new world, settlers substituted by using native corn meal, dubbed "Indian flour", and then flavoring the resulting mush with molasses, the major sweetener used in that period. That mush became known as Indian pudding, and it is traditionally served on Thanksgiving.

I have made this many times in the past ten years, choosing not to make it at Thanksgiving due to the competition of all those pies.

Durgin-Park's Indian Pudding

Preheat oven to 250 degrees

INGREDIENTS: *1 cup cornmeal*
½ cup molasses
¼ cup sugar
¼ cup butter (in the past lard was used)
½ teaspoon salt
¼ teaspoon baking soda
2 eggs, well-beaten
1 and ½ quarts whole milk (6 cups)

Mix together all ingredients with half of the milk that has been heated to just below boiling. Place in a well-buttered 4-quart stone crock or heavy casserole dish and bake in a slow oven till it boils. Then stir in remaining half of the hot milk. It then takes 5 to 7 hours to bake. The secret of its excellence lies in very slow cooking. The longer the pudding bakes the darker and thicker it gets. It's done when it holds its shape on a spoon. Serve with heavy cream, or a more up-to-date addition of a scoop of vanilla ice cream. Serves 8

Alternate "quicker-cooking" version: Preheat oven to 325 degrees. In a medium bowl, combine cornmeal, molasses, sugar, butter, salt, and baking soda. In large saucepan, heat 4 cups of the milk till hot. Gradually whisk the hot milk into the cornmeal mixture. Pour pudding mixture into the saucepan. Cook over moderate heat, stirring, until it boils, thickens, and becomes creamy, about 15 minutes. Stir in beaten eggs. Pour into buttered crock or deep casserole dish and bake in middle of oven for 1 and ¼ hours. Do not cover. Pour the remaining 2 cups of hot milk into the pudding as it bakes, stirring well, baking about 2 hours longer.

Comment from Lorinda R. *I made the Indian pudding in the Crockpot and it was great. I cooked it 5-6 hours, let it set, and then served for dessert, YUM. I'm warming the leftovers tomorrow for friends.*

Comment from Patty C. *I enjoyed reading about Durgin Park and the Indian pudding; it brought back memories of the meals we enjoyed there. I remember the waitresses carrying heavy trays of dishes in one hand, and a heavy water pitcher in the other. We had fun sitting at picnic tables, laughing and talking with strangers.*

It's a cold December day and I'm making the pudding in a Crockpot as I daydream.

Pumpkin Soup with Curry and Mushrooms

This is a wonderful choice for a first course. Whether you are a new cook or an expert, your guests will be dazzled.

INGREDIENTS: *½ pound fresh mushrooms (canned is not good in this recipe), cut in bite-size pieces.*

½ cup chopped onion

2 tablespoons butter

2 tablespoons flour

½ to 1 teaspoon curry powder

3 cups vegetable broth (from cooking carrots and/or potatoes, or store-bought)

1 can (15 ounce) solid pack pumpkin (2 cups if fresh)

1 can (12 ounce) evaporated milk

1 tablespoon honey

¼ teaspoon ground nutmeg – freshly ground if you have whole nutmeg.

½ teaspoon salt

¼ teaspoon pepper

In a large saucepan, sauté the mushrooms and onion in butter until tender. Stir in flour and curry powder until blended. Slowly add the broth while stirring, for about 2 minutes or until thickened. Add pumpkin, milk, honey, salt and pepper, and nutmeg. Simmer (do not boil) until good and hot. Serves 6

Comment from Marianne L.

I saw your Pumpkin Mushroom Curry soup recipe in the paper and made it for supper tonight. My son and husband loved it so much I had to tell you. I am going to make it for Thanksgiving this year. I shredded the mushrooms in my food processor and liked it. Thanks for a wonderful recipe.

Comment from Anne, Haverhill   *My family and I especially liked the Pumpkin Curry Soup, thank you for a really good recipe.*

CRANBERRY CHUTNEY

I have had many raves about this chutney, people pleasantly surprised as to how good it is. Even if you are die-hard fans of cranberry sauce, you will also like the homemade flavor of this deliciously spiced chutney.

INGREDIENTS: *1 (12 ounce) bag fresh or frozen cranberries*
1 cup chopped granny smith apple
1 cup raisins (mix dark and golden raisins if you like)
1 cup chopped onion
1 cup sugar
1 cup white vinegar
¾ cup chopped celery and ¾ cup water
2 teaspoons ground cinnamon
1 ½ teaspoons ground ginger
¼ teaspoon ground cloves

Combine all in a large saucepan and bring to a boil. Reduce heat, simmer uncovered for at least 30 minutes or until slightly thick, stirring occasionally. It will take longer if you double the recipe. Best served slightly warm or room temperature; Keeps well in the refrigerator and can be made 2-3 days ahead. Makes about 4 cups

Comment from Paula, Lawrence   *I loved your Thanksgiving recipes; the chutney was delicious and I had many compliments.*

Jackman's Carry on Stuffing Tradition

My grandparents were known to everyone as Ma and Pa. This is Ma's Oyster Stuffing which we know she made every Thanksgiving from the early 1940s. Their youngest son Robert and his wife Jane continued the tradition for more than sixty years, and then their youngest son Paul accepted the gauntlet, making it every Thanksgiving to this day.

Married to Bob in 1948, Jane tells us of her first Thanksgiving with the Jackman family:

"There were many there, that's for sure, with six brothers, two sisters, and their own family members.

I came from a family that used very few spices; mostly salt and pepper, cinnamon/sugar on toast, and Bell's seasoning in regular stuffing was what I was used to, I was surprised to see fresh Oysters going into a stuffing. Apparently oysters were an important part of the Jackman family Thanksgiving; what a sight when I saw them in the container. Most of the brothers and Pa were anxious to eat some raw, so the oysters were put into small dishes with a shake of salt and pepper and a sprinkle of apple cider vinegar. I was leery but saw they "went down" quickly; I decided to try a small one and lived through it!

Oyster stuffing has been on our Thanksgiving table for our 65 years together. Even the 34 years we lived in Alaska we would use canned oysters; my son Paul actually prefers the slightly stronger flavor they impart." Jane Jackman

Oyster Stuffing – Courtesy of Jane Jackman

INGREDIENTS: *1 pint fresh oysters with juice*
½ pound (2 sticks) butter
1 large loaf white bread, broken into small pieces
Salt and pepper to taste

Put raw oysters with juice into a large pan, adding butter until melted. Cook only until the edges curl; **over cooking** will ruin them. Add bread, salt and pepper to taste and any additional water needed for the consistency you prefer. We like a fairly moist stuffing which warms up easily when re-heating; will stuff a 20 pound turkey.

Turkey Terrific Pita Sandwich

The day after Thanksgiving is different to everyone, but most of us do not want to cook. If that is you and you have leftover turkey this is a delicious way to use it up. My family looked forward to a turkey sandwich late in the evening on Thanksgiving, usually after playing cards (Pitch), or a scrabble game, and we were content with turkey, a layer of stuffing, but the" Dilly-Dali-Deli" in Tewksbury, MA, now closed, took a turkey sandwich up a notch, enough to become well known for what they named the "Turkey Terrific". You had to order by 10 am to bypass long lines. Our office was nearby, and that sandwich became a lunch favorite for several years.

How to make: Cut in half a large pita pocket (whole wheat or white); spread mayonnaise inside, and don't be skimpy. In this order layer: stuffing, jellied cranberry sauce, liberal amount of sliced turkey right from the bird, (salt and pepper to taste on stuffing and turkey), and shredded lettuce. On the side place a "half-sour" pickle.

Add a slice of pumpkin-nut bread, and continue to enjoy Thanksgiving.

December: Christmas — Most Meaningful

I am grateful for so many wonderful Christmas's, especially those I enjoyed with my children. Favorite memories are shopping for just the right gifts, family visiting, the house decorated, luminaries lining the front of the house for our very special Christmas Eve and of course all the cooking and baking.

Then there were the special Christmas's when I wrote a local food column; new recipes, many new friends, those readers who shared their Holiday traditions and "favorite things" with me. Those years also left me with many special and delightful memories.

Yet what humbles me are the Christmas's that my parents provided us eight children during our growing-up years. They both worked two jobs to do it. My mother spent all day being a mother, and cooking and cleaning, then from six to eleven many evenings working as a waitress, on her feet the entire time. My father worked nights on the loading docks of a trucking company and days driving a school bus and working in his huge garden. Their hard work provided Christmas mornings with several gifts for each child to open, always one big gift of skates, a new bike, or a beautiful doll lamp. Then there were the Christmas dinners with turkey, two kinds of stuffing, fresh ground cranberry orange relish, bowls of fruit and nuts to crack, and a loaded pie and dessert table.

Of all the Christmas's in my life, those are the most meaningful.

STANDING RIB ROAST WITH ROASTED POTATOES

Preheat oven to 475 degrees

INGREDIENTS, SEASONING RUB:
1 tablespoon fresh rosemary leaves, chopped
1 tablespoon fresh thyme leaves
2 garlic cloves, chopped fine
1 and ½ teaspoons coarse kosher salt
1 teaspoon fresh ground black pepper

*3-Rib standing beef rib roast (about 8 ½ pounds),
     with all but ¼ inch layer of fat removed
2 tablespoons olive oil
Potatoes: 5 pounds russet baking potatoes, about 10;
     salt, pepper, paprika, ½ cup chopped parsley.*

Place roast, ribs side down, in center of roasting pan, 18x12x2 inches. Rub oil on top and sides of beef. Combine seasoning rub ingredients and rub mixture on top and sides of beef. Roast beef in lower third of oven for 20 minutes. Meanwhile, peel potatoes and halve crosswise. After 20 minutes remove roast from oven and skim all but ½ cup fat from pan with a bulb baster or spoon. Arrange potatoes around beef and turn with tongs to coast with drippings. Season potatoes with salt, pepper, and paprika. Reduce heat to 350 degrees and roast beef for about 1 ½ hours, or until meat thermometer inserted in fleshy part of beef registers 130 degrees for medium-rare. Turn potatoes occasionally to brown. When done, transfer to a platter, cover loosely with foil, and let rest 15 minutes; if sliced too soon, the juices will run out. When done, toss potatoes with chopped parsley and pan drippings.

SHITAKE MUSHROOM GRAVY COMES HIGHLY RECOMMENDED

This delicious gravy/sauce recipe was sent to me by my niece Janine and her husband Paul. They are both Naval Officers who have made a wonderful life with each other, the Navy, and their extended families and friends they have met on their journey.

In Janine's own words she explains how she first came across this recipe:

"The recipe actually comes from shared Holiday meals when stationed in Guantanamo Bay, Cuba 1996-1999;

I honestly do not remember who first introduced me to it to give proper credit but it was the first gravy that I actually liked (not normally a gravy fan). I personalized the recipe to our taste by adding more mushrooms and rosemary. It goes well with turkey, pork, and especially beef.

"Gitmo" (as it is called by Military Personnel), is a unique place as you cannot leave the base so holidays are celebrated with many different people, often on the beach as it is always summer like, and you can't help but be introduced to many types of foods and traditions. We have some of our fondest memories from there as we live by the motto; "Home is where the Navy sends you!" Janine D. Allen, CAPT, NC, USN

Shitake Mushroom Gravy – Recipe courtesy of Janine D. Allen, my eldest Jackman niece

Here is gravy with a rich flavor suited for special occasions and holidays. Cream sherry takes it up a notch.

Janine and Paul add that it would also make a good base for a soup.

INGREDIENTS: *½ cup all-purpose flour*
½ cup dry sherry
3 tablespoons butter
12 ounces shitake mushrooms, (sliced, can add more, it will just be more chunky)
1 tablespoon plus 1 teaspoon fresh rosemary, (pull off stems, leave whole or chop, add more if you like rosemary)
4 cups chicken broth

1/3 cup whipping cream
2 teaspoons dried thyme
2 teaspoons dried tarragon

Blend flour and sherry into a smooth paste, set aside. Melt butter in large sauce pan, add mushrooms and rosemary. Sauté for 3 minutes. Transfer pan juices (if you have any) into large glass bowl. Spoon off fat and add enough chicken broth to make 4-5 cups of liquid. Add to sauce pan. Whisk in flour paste until smooth. Boil until thickened, about 10 minutes. Mix in cream, thyme and tarragon. Season with salt and pepper.

This goes with most everything from ham to chicken, but wonderful on a rib-eye steak or prime rib.

Peppermint Bark

Crushed peppermint candy gives this chocolate bark a festive look and a seasonal taste. I always have to double the recipe. Great for an office party, candy swap, school class party, and homemade gift-giving.

INGREDIENTS: *12 ounces high quality semi-sweet chocolate*
1 pound white chocolate with cocoa butter
½ teaspoon peppermint extract
½ to ¾ cup candy canes or peppermint candy, crushed

Line a 15x10 inch jelly roll pan with foil extended over sides. Grease foil with non-stick spray.

Melt chocolate chips in a double boiler over medium-low heat. Pour evenly into pan and smooth with spatula. Sprinkle with about one-quarter cup peppermint candy. Place in refrigerator until firm.

Heat white chocolate chips in a double boiler over medium-low heat until chocolate is almost melted. Remove insert from pan and stir until completely melted. Stir in extract. Cool slightly. Pour over chocolate layer and spread quickly to cover. Sprinkle with one-half cup crushed candy. Chill until both layers are firm. Lift foil out of pan and shake off excess candy. Peel foil gently from bottom of candy. Trim edges and cut into 2 inch squares.

Note: When I made this I did not use as much crushed peppermint candy as the recipe called for.

Comment from Sharon, Methuen: *I made the Peppermint Bark and it was GREAT. I used less crushed peppermint and my husband (not a peppermint fan) loved it. This is a keeper and will be a Christmas tradition.*

GINGERBREAD COOKIE CUTOUTS

My mother made these cookies every Christmas for her grandchildren. Whether you use this recipe or your favorite put on some Christmas music and bring some young children into your kitchen for an afternoon of cookie baking and memory making.

INGREDIENTS: *1 cup butter, softened*
¼ cup sugar
½ cup brown sugar
½ cup molasses
1 egg
3 ¼ cups flour
1 teaspoon baking soda
¾ teaspoon baking powder
1 teaspoon salt
2 teaspoons ginger
1 teaspoon cinnamon

¼ teaspoon allspice

In large bowl cream butter and sugars until fluffy; add molasses and egg, mixing well. In a separate bowl mix together the remaining dry ingredients. Add 1/3 at a time to creamed ingredients, mixing well. Cover with plastic wrap and refrigerate 1 hour for easier handling. Preheat oven to 350 degrees.

On a floured surface, roll out dough, 1/4 at a time, to 1/8 " thickness; cut with floured gingerbread boy and girl cookie cutters (or any desired shape). Keep remaining dough chilled. Place 1 inch apart on ungreased cookie sheet, bake 6 to 9 minutes or until set; cool 1 minute and remove from cookie sheets.

Frosting:

Combine 2 cups white confectioners' sugar, 1/3 cup soft butter, ½ teaspoon vanilla, and 1 to 2 tablespoons half & half or milk, beat until smooth. Pipe frosting onto cookies to outline, or spread to cover cookie; use raisins, mini chocolate chips or small candies for eyes and buttons; makes approximately 2 dozen cookies.

PECAN PIE COOKIE-BARS

Cookie crust: Preheat oven to 350 degrees. Spray a 15x10x1 inch baking pan with cooking spray. In large bowl with mixer at medium speed beat 3 cups flour, 1 cup cold butter (no substitute) cut into pieces, ½ cup sugar, and ½ teaspoon salt until mixture resembles fine crumbs; press firmly into prepared pan. Bake 20 minutes or until light golden brown.

Filling: While crust is in oven, in a large bowl beat 4 eggs, 1 ½ cups light corn syrup, 1 ½ cups sugar, 3 tablespoons melted butter, and 1 ½ teaspoons vanilla extract, until well blended. Stir in 2 ½ cups pecans chopped into large pieces. Immediately pour this over the baked hot crust, spreading evenly. Bake 25 minutes or until filling is firm around edges and slightly firm in center. Cool completely before cutting; Makes 48, 2½ inch bars.

HANUKKAH

Hanukkah falling on Thanksgiving will not happen again for 77,000 years

Thursday November 28, 2013 the first day of Hanukkah (Jewish festival of lights) was on Thanksgiving, the American festival of giving thanks. The last time this happened was in 1888 and will not happen again in our lifetimes.

In many homes, the expectations for meals are usually pretty rigid for both of these celebrations.

My thoughts strayed to how families blend these long-standing traditions on a daily basis, maintaining and honoring beliefs and ideals that can be so different.

I believe it is compromise; whatever tradition each family has, it's all about family.

You honor each other's traditions by understanding the family coming together.

Hanukkah and Thanksgiving are two important holidays that bring families together. As you gather around the dinner table, bring your own stories to the holiday. Make time to tell these stories, recounting times that "light" came unexpectedly and exuberantly into your lives. The latter refers to the Hanukkah tradition of lights, but it will pertain to everyone in some way, it is blending.

As far as food is concerned, both holidays are filled with traditions rather than hard rules. So on Thanksgiving itself, bring a little Hanukkah spirit to your traditional Thanksgiving dinner by serving sweet potato latkes with a cranberry-apple sauce alongside the turkey. Add "Carrot Cupcakes", a treat for the children, to your dessert table; the sweet potatoes and carrots will fit right in with the Thanksgiving theme.

If you are thinking of making sufganiyot, traditional Hanukkah doughnuts, make the traditional yeast dough with the addition of canned pumpkin, which adds great flavor and color; warm homemade pumpkin doughnuts-so tempting to make, and eat, even as I write this.

Other suggestions include making a stuffing made of challah bread, perhaps a sweet potato kugel. One suggestion that sounds tempting to me are potato latkes with a horseradish sauce and smoked turkey on the side; a delicious blending of foods as well as families.

SWEET POTATO AND SCALLION LATKES

INGREDIENTS: *1 large white potato, russet the best, peeled and grated (Sweet potatoes have little starch, the starch in the russet potatoes helps to hold the latke together.)*

2 large sweet potatoes peeled and grated. (2 lbs. sweet potatoes makes a generous 7 cups grated)

6 scallions, white and light green parts, thinly sliced

4 tablespoons flour

2 eggs, lightly beaten

¼ teaspoon of each; salt and black pepper

¾ cup of safflower or peanut oil, divided (I prefer the flavor of peanut oil)

In large bowl, combine grated sweet potatoes with scallion slices, flour, eggs, salt, and pepper. Mix until well combined. In a large heavy frying pan, heat ¼ cup of the oil until small amount of latke mixture sizzle when added (1-2 minutes). Drop spoonfuls (about one-eighth cup) of batter into pan, flattening with a slotted spatula. Cook until one side is browned, about 2 minutes, and then cook other side until brown and crisp, 1-2 minutes more; cook as many at a time as will fit comfortably in the pan. The first ¼ cup oil should make about 15 latkes. Remove cooked latkes with spatula to a cookie sheet lined with paper towels to absorb excess oil. Keep warm in a low oven until ready to serve. After 15 latkes are finished, pour ¼ cup oil into the pan and make another 15. Pour remaining ¼ cup oil in pan to cook the last 15. Makes 45 latkes Serve warm with bowls of applesauce, plain yogurt, or sour cream.

CHAPTER 4
INTRODUCTION TRAVELING, BRINGING HOME THE RECIPES

I have been fortunate to have taken trips to Alaska, Bogotá, Bolivia, Buenos Aires, Uruguay, Munich, as well as destinations here in the states. When writing my food column, I brought back a traditional recipe from each city. I share those recipes here and tell of experiences, people and cultures that awed me; a fish-wheel on the Copper River in Alaska, attending a five-star wedding in Bogota (I could have been on 5th Avenue), experiencing a traditional "Asado" in Montevideo, and seeing the Tango done artfully in Argentina. Several recipes are true comfort foods of that country, as is the Beer Coffee Cake from Munich's Bavarian section that is very popular at the Oktoberfest celebration each year.

An excerpt from Alaska trip:" We ended our trip taking home a treasure chest; a huge cooler packed with 50 lbs. of halibut and salmon from Jane's freezer. Carrying our treasure, we walked into Anchorage airport and "dotting" the floor were many "duct-taped coolers" going home with travelers, holding a bounty of Copper River Reds."

RECIPES:
SALMON CHOWDER
AJIACO; NATIVE TRADITIONAL DISH
CHANTILLY LEMON WHIP
FILLET OF BEEF ARGENTINE

GERMAN BEER COFFEE CAKE
MIKE J's PIZZA
CHIMICHURRI; URUGUAYAN WAY
VEGETARIAN PAD THAI
FRIED GREEN TOMATO BLT
VANILLA CRÈME' BRULEE'

TRAVELING & BRINGING HOME THE RECIPES, THANK YOU FAMILY

How blessed am I! When my family were in different parts of the world, or even in another state; they always welcomed me and made sure I didn't miss out on a fantastic and wondrous place to see. I never would have been able to travel to Europe, South America and Alaska without my family's encouragement. Here and right now, I want to thank all of them for their unselfishness, always making me feel welcome and special, and taking time away from their lives to make sure I saw the sights and experienced the flavors of wherever I was. I thank you for the wonderful memories I have, and am so grateful to you; here is what you gave me!

FISH WHEELS, FAMILY, AND SALMON; I'M IN ALASKA

I arrived in Copper Center, four hours East of Anchorage (affectionately called Los Anchorage by residents), anxious to see my Aunt and Uncle who moved to Alaska in the 1970's. Teachers, their focus was to educate the Eskimo and Inuit families living in remote villages of the northern wilderness. For years Jane and Bob experienced poor living conditions in order to bring basic education to those with no access to schools or public facilities. Their efforts were tireless, experiences many and vast, their memories and stories very interesting.

Eventually they settled in Copper Center and my oldest son Mark and I were finally visiting.

I learned a lot about salmon and how it was caught. They have a fish-wheel on the river, which looks roughly like a paddle boat/mini Ferris wheel. This sits in the water, close to shore, with a dock for easy access from land. The river is dotted with many fish wheels on each side, usually co-owned by several families, who share the "catch". The wheel turns and catches the salmon as they swim up river, anywhere's from fifty to two hundred and fifty pounds daily during the salmon runs which average three weeks in June and again in late July. Alaskans call sockeye salmon "Copper River Reds", the most prevalent. King salmon, called Coho's, are not as plentiful. Most families need two large freezers to accommodate all the salmon, halibut, and game that are common eating in Alaska homes.

We ended our trip taking home a treasure chest; a huge cooler packed with fifty pounds of halibut and salmon from Jane's freezer. Carrying our treasure, we walked into Anchorage airport and saw many "duct-taped coolers" going home with travelers, holding a bounty of Copper River Reds.

Comments from Sue & Bob B: *I greatly enjoyed reading about your Alaska trip. My wife and I both love salmon and I have been contemplating a trip to Alaska with either a fishing party or just us on a majestic tour with salmon fishing. If we were to go to the Copper River area, do you know of groups that offer trips, and what is considered the best salmon type?*

Answer: My family in Alaska helped me with answers for you. Alaskans call sockeye salmon "copper river reds", the most prevalent. King salmon, called Coho's, are not as plentiful. The first salmon run is in early June lasting about three weeks. The second run is in late July.

Salmon run along the sides of the river so many people fish from shore. A fishing license is required. The MILEPOST magazine is an Alaska travel planner. It will give you all the information you need. Have fun, Pat

One of Jane's most popular recipes, this creamy chowder is loaded with vegetables and hits the spot on a cold winter day, and many Alaska days are -25 degrees.

Salmon Chowder – Courtesy Jane Jackman, Copper Center, AK

INGREDIENTS: *2 cups salmon cooked, or 2 cups canned salmon*
1 clove garlic, minced
3 tablespoons butter
½ cup chopped onion
½ cup chopped celery
¼ cup chopped green pepper
2 cups chicken broth
1 cup diced carrots
1 cup diced potatoes
½ cup diced zucchini
1 cup of frozen corn or peas
1 ½ teaspoons salt
½ teaspoon thyme (key to the flavor)
¾ teaspoon black pepper

1 can evaporated milk (using canned milk was necessary as the nearest

supermarket was a four hour drive made once a month), and it makes the chowder creamy and delicious.

In a large pot lightly sauté garlic, onion, celery and green pepper in butter. Add broth, carrots, potatoes, zucchini, corn and salmon; add more broth if too thick. Add seasonings and simmer for 30 minutes. Add evaporated milk and simmer another 20-30 minutes; Makes 6 servings.

Comment from Dick T.: *I'm 79 years of age and still like to cook on occasion, and one recipe is your salmon" chowdah" which is great. I make it ahead and have it for a few meals; it's easy to make.*

Comment from Margaret B: *Simply put the Salmon Chowder was delicious!*

Question from Lori M: *I am making chowder soon and wanted to ask you about evaporated milk. A friend always uses that when making her chowders. What do you recommend?*

Response: Coming from a large family, I grew up on corn chowder and fish chowder. My mother and grandmother used evaporated milk in their chowders (evaporated milk is whole milk with water removed). I believe evaporated milk was used for economic reasons (keeps well and less costly), BUT… many cooks discovered it is a bit of a thickener and makes a good tasting chowder. The added flavors of onion and salt pork are keys. If you prefer, substitute with whole milk or half & half.

BOGOTA, COLOMBIA AND A GRAND WEDDING

The year is 2000, and attending a wedding in Bogota was a study of contrasts. There were dangers to be considered as several American women had been kidnapped in recent years. There were three women attending the wedding from America and the utmost precautions were taken to protect the groom's mother, sister-in-law, and myself. We each had an armed guard with us at all times, and travelled together in a SUV.

But all of that didn't bother me at all; I was there to watch a very special man, my nephew, marry his beautiful Colombian fiancée, whom I have grown to love dearly. That evening we were chauffeured down a long torch-lit drive to a sweeping estate-like venue, first to witness the marriage of Chris to Maria Claudia in a lovely Spanish style mission church, warm and bright with flowers and candles. Following the wedding, our escorts, in tails and white gloves, escorted us up a grand stairway and into a festive ball-room. This was Cinderella-like and with no exaggeration was the closest I ever came to a Fifth-avenue wedding; spectacular gowns, colorful firs, and huge vats of roses everywhere; truly exquisite and I found the people of Bogota to be warm and hospitable, making us feel welcome and at home every minute.

This stew took a starring role in Maria and Chris's pre-wedding supper hosted by Maria's Aunt and held in her beautiful home which stood high on a Bogota hillside. This is a traditional Colombian favorite, a comfort food served often to family and guests.

AJIACO (PRONOUNCED AH-HEE-AH-KO), A CHICKEN, CORN AND POTATO STEW NATIVE TO COLUMBIA

INGREDIENTS: *1 chicken, about 3 ½ pounds and 2 quarts water*
2 cups reduced sodium chicken broth
1 large onion, chopped
1 tablespoon dried "guascas" or oregano
1 ½ teaspoons salt
1 pound papas criollas (thawed if you have found in the freezer section of store) or 1 pound russet potatoes

1 pound yukon gold potatoes, peeled and cut into 1 inch pieces

1 pound red potatoes, peeled and cut into 1 inch pieces

3 ears of corn cut into 1 inch pieces OR 2 cups of whole kernel corn

1 cup creama or ½ cup heavy cream mixed with ½ cup sour cream

¼ cup drained capers

3 ripe avocados cut into small cubes

¼ cup chopped cilantro (to cook in stew) and extra to serve as garnish

Put chicken in an 8 quart soup-pot with water, broth, onion, oregano, and salt. Bring to a boil, skimming off the foam. Reduce heat and simmer till cooked through, about 45 minutes. Transfer chicken to a plate to cool. Add papas criollas to broth, or peeled and coarsely grated russet potatoes (done quick in a blender). Simmer uncovered, about 30 minutes, till potatoes are falling apart and thickening the broth (mash if necessary). Add all remaining potatoes, simmer, covered, about 20 minutes till tender. Add corn, 1/4 cup cilantro, and 1 teaspoon freshly ground black pepper, continue to simmer. Coarsely shred chicken, add to stew; cook till hot and bubbly. Serve stew with "creama" (heavy cream), capers, avocados, and chopped cilantro as garnishes.

FASCINATING LAPAZ, BOLIVIA

Known as the most Indian country in South America; I witnessed the culture and customs first hand. I was quite excited when I was invited to come to this country. My nephew was working for our State Department in the American Embassy in La Paz and he and his family looked forward to seeing people from home. First, I had to acclimate myself to the very high altitude; walking slow with no quick movements was necessary for a few days. After that I enjoyed their beautiful home and the sights that Bolivia has to offer, such as the center of La Paz with the Government Palace, and a magnificent Cathedral. We toured Tiwanaku, a site of pre-Incan civilization with visible ruins that have been excavated; nothing short of amazing to view what had once been a village and home to many.

Shopping in the Open Air Markets is not to be missed. I brought home gifts of hand knitted Alpaca wool (so soft) scarves, a complete hand-painted chess set with hand carved pieces, and a beautiful Alpaca jacket. Bolivia is a poor country but amazing to see how talented the people are in creating such beautiful things.

When strolling through the open air markets in La Paz, you can find numerous vendors selling Chantilly, a refreshing dessert, quick to make, and popular.

CHANTILLY (LEMON WHIP)

INGREDIENTS: *1 (12oz) can evaporated milk, well chilled (low fat <u>not</u> recommended, too watery)*
Juice from one lemon
½ cup granulated sugar (regular sugar needed to produce fluffy volume)

For best results use electric mixer; chill bowl, beaters, and milk. In a large bowl beat chilled evaporated milk with mixer on high until milk is light and airy like whipped cream. Slowly drizzle in lemon juice, continuing to whip. Slowly add sugar continuing to whip; mix until sugar is absorbed. If the whip starts to revert back to liquid, beat again with electric mixer. Serve alone or with berries, makes 6 servings.

BUENOS AIRES! YES, I'M IN ARGENTINA

This is a city with a very European feel to it. On one corner you see a glimpse of Paris, and nearby, beautiful Italian architecture. To get properly acquainted my brother suggested a four-hour professional tour. The four areas of Buenos Aries include a very upscale area of expensive shops and magnificent Opera House. Another area is where many people from Italy settled; now so large they may soon have their own town government. It is very colorful and artsy with murals painted on many buildings. I loved the open air music and dancing; watching couples perform the tango; some in jeans, some in authentic costumes.

The waterfront section (Puerta Madera), is where we enjoyed a wonderful dinner followed by a stroll along the mile-long waterfront with its twenty-foot wide cobblestone walkway and ritzy shops.

The fourth area is the City Square where the Presidential Palace is, painted pink in its entirety. I was humbled by the Circle of Doves, a symbolic monument created by mothers of deceased soldiers, very poignant.

One very different custom is that restaurants close from four pm to eight pm. Even in private homes the evening meal starts much later than what our custom is.

We drove out to the country-side of Buenos Aires to spend a day at a Gaucho Ranch. As we arrived what I saw reminded me of the ranch on the old television show "Dallas"; beautiful rolling green fields that surrounded a sprawling ranch house, white fencing going on forever, and I estimate about one-hundred horses in a corral. We were greeted by staff in authentic Uruguayan cowboy dress serving us wine and hot empanadas, a delicious meat pie. We were told our day would be filled with horseback and wagon rides, trick riding, an impressive five course barbecue, a stage show and dancing; FUN!

Another wonderful event was our evening at an upscale supper club, *"Senor Tango"*. We walked in to see mirrored ceilings, red velvet walls, fresh flowers galore, and tiny white lights covering everything. We enjoyed an elegant meal as we sat surrounding a huge center stage where a two-hour show told the story of how the tango had evolved from its beginning in Argentina to the present day. There was also a wonderful part of the show that told the story of the Argentine cowboy and Indians, which included two horses and riders going onstage. The club was dark, smoke rising, and very solemn; breathtaking.

Many of the restaurants we ate in have an Old World feel and often you could find your beef sizzling in an outdoor pit. Argentina is known for raising and serving great tasting beef; we were not disappointed.

Fillet of Beef Argentine

INGREDIENTS: *1 beef tenderloin, 3 pounds*
                     ¼ cup butter
                     2 hard-cooked egg yolks, mashed
                     ½ cup finely chopped mushrooms
                     2 tablespoons chopped scallions (green onions)
                     2 tablespoons olive oil
                     ½ cup red wine
                     ½ cup beef stock or bouillon
                     ½ teaspoon of each: dried thyme and paprika.
                     1 onion, thinly sliced

Heat butter in a skillet, brown beef evenly then place in a shallow roasting pan. Add egg yolks, mushrooms, and scallions to butter left in skillet; blend to make a paste; add oil if needed and spread over beef; Salt and pepper to taste. Pour in wine, beef stock, seasonings and onion. Place in a 325 degree oven; roast 20-25 minutes per pound for rare or 140 degrees on meat thermometer. Turn beef once during roasting. When done remove to a warm platter to rest for 10 minutes; cover with aluminum foil tent to keep warm. Slice beef in 1 inch portions. Serves 6-8

MUNICH, GERMANY AND NEIGHBORING SALZBURG, AUSTRIA

I'm off to Frankfurt in the Bavarian section of Germany to visit my nephew Mike and his wife Heather. Their three-year assignment for the State Department was coming to an end and they were urging me to visit. Frankfurt is a cultural town known as the financial center of Europe. The harbor, along the "Main River", is an area where people were jogging, reading, listening to music, and just relaxing. Minutes from the harbor to downtown, we people watched from an outdoor café while I admired the pretty Swiss-like architecture all around me, (not to miss the Starbuck's on the corner). Interesting, was seeing many bicycles parked in racks on most every street corner; obviously a popular mode of transportation (understandably with $8 /gallon for gas).

Soon we were driving to Salzburg Austria for an overnight stay. There were signs everywhere that this is a very musical city, where Mozart was born and music an integral piece. I was drawn to the gorgeous gardens and another magnificent huge Cathedral, much like St. Peter's in Rome. Mike accompanied me on the Sound of Music Tour which included a scenic ride into the mountains, and the beautiful church where the wedding scene was filmed, I'm sure chosen due to its grand architecture.

I recalled my visit of a few months back to the Trapp Family Lodge in Stowe Vermont; and what I experienced there and saw here all came together magnificently.

Munich was next and an absolute favorite city of mine. This is an enjoyable and fascinating place, and though we had just a few days, Mike made sure we saw a lot. We walked and ate our way through that city, and I loved every minute of it. We enjoyed the world famous Hofbrauhaus beer hall with its live German polka music blasting, people dancing in the aisles, and beer and huge fresh-baked pretzels in abundance. My next trip to Munich will be for the Oktoberfest celebration when close to six million revelers crowd this city and area to celebrate Bavarian culture.

This old German recipe blends spices, nuts, and dates with beer; Lowenbrau or Becks are suggestions. Prettily baked in a tube or Bundt pan, generously sprinkled with powdered sugar, you will enjoy a "piece" of Bavarian culture

GERMAN BEER COFFEE CAKE

Preheat oven to 350 degrees

INGREDIENTS: *2 cups packed dark brown sugar*
1 cup butter, softened
2 eggs
1 teaspoon cinnamon
½ teaspoon allspice
½ teaspoon ground cloves
3 cups all-purpose flour, sifted (use a whisk to aerate flour and omit sifting)
2 teaspoons baking soda

½ teaspoon salt
1 cup chopped walnuts
2 cups chopped dates
2 cups beer (German beer preferable)
Powdered sugar (white confectioners' sugar)

Combine brown sugar and butter in a mixing bowl; cream until smooth and well-blended. Add eggs, one at a time, beating well after each addition. Sift cinnamon, allspice, cloves, flour, baking soda, and salt together. Dust walnuts and dates with a small amount of this mixture. Add remaining flour mixture alternately with beer to creamed mixture, blending well after each addition. Stir in walnuts and dates; Spoon batter into a large, well-buttered and floured, tube or Bundt pan.

Bake 1 hour and 15 minutes or until cake tester comes out clean. Let stand 5 minutes, invert onto a wire rack. Sprinkle with powdered sugar when cool and place on a serving plate.

Oktoberfest tidbit: "Did you know?" 220,000 is the number of stolen beer mugs recovered by security during a recent Oktoberfest celebration in Munich.

Along with being incredible hosts who made this trip so memorable, Mike and Heather also like to cook. Mike made this pizza from scratch, and it was so fresh tasting and delicious that I need to include it with my memories of my trip to Germany and share it with others. And what could go better with that ice cold German beer?

Mike J's Pizza (Will make one large or two small pizzas)

CRUST:
- *3 ½ cups all-purpose flour, may substitute wheat flour as desired*
- *2 packets yeast*
- *1 ½ cups warm water*
- *1 tablespoons sugar*

Combine dry ingredients. Add water, mix into dough, kneading until not sticky (may have to add sprinkling of flour), knead and form into a ball. Place in greased bowl on a warm surface, cover with damp towel. Rise to double size.

SAUCE:
- *1 (32 ounce) can tomato sauce*
- *1 (15 ounce) can tomato paste*
- *1/3 cup parmesan or Romano cheese*
- *1 ½ tablespoons minced garlic*
- *1 tablespoon sugar*
- *Add spices to your taste (choice of oregano, thyme, sage, rosemary, crushed red pepper)*

Combine all ingredients except sugar and cheese. Cook on medium heat 15 minutes, stirring constantly.

Then simmer for 2 hours, stirring occasionally; add sugar and cheese last 15 minutes of simmer.

Make pizza: Roll out or pat dough to edge of pizza pan. Spread on a thin layer of sun-dried tomato **or** basil pesto. Ladle on 2 cups of sauce spreading out to crust edge.

Sauté until softened all or any: chopped onion, green pepper, pieces

cooked chicken, sun dried tomatoes, place on pizza. Top with cheese; 2 cups shredded mozzarella and ½ cup shredded sharp cheddar.
Bake in preheated oven at 400 degrees 10 minutes or until cheese melted and crust lightly browned.

Montevideo, Uruguay; Enjoying an "Asado" (traditional Uruguayan barbecue)

Our first full day in Uruguay was a trip to Punta Del Este, an ocean-side Resort dotted with gorgeous condominiums and five- star restaurants. We enjoyed a spectacular seafood dinner on the patio with fruit laden sangria that I have tried to duplicate several times. Then I salivated as we shopped at Gucci, Armani, and Polo stores.

The next evening Maria Claudia and Chris hosted a traditional Uruguayan barbecue at their home.

These are Events, usually hiring two to four people to cook the many courses. This day Chris did all the cooking and superbly. The barbecue pit is housed in their poolside Guest House in a comfortable family room.

The cooking area alone is about 5 ft x 3 ft and only wood is used. Chris explained that the preparation is part of the party; often a family member has a guitar and will play traditional songs. Friends and family linger by the grill enjoying a glass of wine, the aroma, and the fire crackling away. We aimed to please, grabbed our wine, and enjoyed six courses consisting of thick slabs of roasted provolone cheese, three types of sausages, beef tenderloin, suckling pig, chimichurri (a spicy condiment), salads and Maria's baked stuffed potatoes, her mother's traditional Columbian recipe. For us, this was a once in a lifetime treat; more than a meal, and truly an event.

Chimichurri sauce from Uruguay is not meant to be peppery hot; it is more a robust flavor that enhances grilled meats and chicken with its freshness; Also good as a marinade when roasting vegetables.

INGREDIENTS: *1 bunch parsley, chopped fine*

½ cup fresh oregano (remove leaves from stems)

10 cloves garlic, chopped fine

2 seeded red peppers, chopped fine (or ½ teaspoon red pepper flakes) Spanish morrones or red bell peppers good.

¼ cup red wine vinegar

2/3 cup to ¾ cup olive oil

1 teaspoon salt and ½ teaspoon fresh ground black pepper

1 teaspoon sweet smoked paprika

If using a processor, pulse and chop instead of puree, as you do not want a paste.

Finely chop parsley and oregano, garlic and the peppers (or ½ teaspoon dried pepper flakes).

If you are making in the processor chop everything adding parsley last, otherwise it will be paste.

Put everything into a jar and add salt, spices, vinegar and oil.

It is important to rest it for at least 1 hour before using.

CHRISTMAS IN TELLURIDE CO

Our magnificent view.

I never expected to see what I believe to be a crowning achievement in the Rocky Mountains. Telluride is a lovely place on this earth, a small town in a true box canyon, surrounded by straight-up soaring 14,000 foot peaks that are not in the distance, but smack right in your face.

Many hours of our days went by like minutes as we drove through mountain ranges that used to be gold and silver mines. I could see visions of the true west as we saw signs like the old Rio Grande railroad, Smuggler Mining Co, and Tomboy Gold-Mine.

In the late 1800's Telluride had its share of notorious outlaws, and on

Main Street there are still Saloons to enjoy a nice meal while bringing back some of that atmosphere. Walking down Main Street I saw no fast food drive-up, Dunkin Donuts, or even a traffic light. What you see preserves Telluride's legacy of the true Old West and its mining era.

At one time Telluride was close to becoming a ghost town, but the majestic mountains and winter adventures saved it from that fate. Telluride is now a winter wonderland with ski resorts. Telluride Ski Resort encompasses two towns and from the gondola ride I took to the Mountaintop, I witnessed the spectacular view and a five-star après-ski restaurant that Mark and Lisa didn't want me to miss. After skiing or hiking and you are back on Main St., don't miss the line of Tomboy (remember the gold mine?) homemade soaps at Picaya, an emporium-like gift shop where there are distinctive items from around the world. Walk a little further to Honga's Pan Asian restaurant which is funky, chic, and sophisticated.

Pat, Lisa & son, Mark

VEGETARIAN PAD THAI – RECIPE COURTESY OF LISA HORLICK, OWNER OF PICAYA IN TELLURIDE CO

1. Make sauce ahead (keeps well in refrigerator), 2 cups yields 6 to 8 servings (keep warm on stove).

    Sauce ingredients: 2 cups vegetable stock or hot water, 6 tablespoons tamarind concentrate or dried tamarind, ½ cup soy sauce, ½ cup dark brown sugar, 1to2 teaspoons ground cayenne pepper

2. Soak rice noodles only till al dente (pliable), too soft will be mushy. A 16 ounce bag is 6 to 8 servings.

    About 2 cups noodles, loosely packed, is good for 1 serving..

3. Tofu; Use a firm textured tofu cut into thin pieces, a good handful per serving.

4. Prep all ingredients, have at room temperature.

FOR 1 SERVING:*1 full cup bean sprouts*
1 handful green onions, halved lengthwise, cut into 2 inch pieces
1to2 tablespoons chopped dry-roasted peanuts
Good pinch of minced garlic
1 egg

MAKE PAD THAI:

In wok or large deep skillet, heat oil over high heat. Add tofu and garlic; cook till tofu a little crisp. Add 2 cups loosely packed noodles (1 serving) and ladle in about ¼ cup of warm sauce. Stir rigorously, cooking noodles till soft. When noodles are done (taste), push to side, crack 1 egg in middle, let set 10-15 seconds and toss all together. Add bean sprouts, chopped peanuts, and scallions (green onions). Add sauce if too pale. Plate this serving; serve with lime wedge and more peanuts. Give wok a rinse; wipe off excess food bits, put back on heat for next serving. (Always start with a hot wok to smoky point).

MYRTLE BEACH AND CHARLESTON IN MARCH

We wanted to escape New Hampshire in March; the gray snow, slush and mud! My sister Laraine and I joined friends, three Martin sisters, Pat, Mary, and Hazel in Myrtle Beach South Caroline for a six day reprieve from our New Hampshire winter. We were grateful for the beautiful sunny days, and my favorite; early morning walks on the beach. We enjoyed visiting all the tourist attractions, but it was the sun that we reveled in. And then there was the traditional Southern food; shrimp and grits, a BLT with crispy fried green tomatoes, and Purloo (chicken cooked with rice, vegetables, and bacon) all good to me.

Our day drip to Charleston was fantastic. What a beautiful, historic old city. The best way to see it is a three- hour guided tour, where we enjoyed seeing the beautiful old homes of Charleston and the famous harbor with its history of the Civil War which was fascinating to hear.

From Myrtle Beach to Charleston and all through the south, Fried Green Tomatoes are a tradition. What turned me on was the use of these warm, crispy slices in a BLT instead of red tomato; a bit of heaven!

FRIED GREEN TOMATO BLT SANDWICH

INGREDIENTS: *2 large green tomatoes, cored and sliced ½ inch thick*
1 teaspoon sea salt or kosher salt

1 teaspoon freshly ground black pepper
½ cup all purpose flour
½ cup yellow cornmeal
1 large egg
½ cup buttermilk
Peanut oil for frying

Use some of the salt and pepper to season both sides of tomatoes. Mix all dry ingredients in a small bowl. In another bowl, whisk egg and buttermilk. Pour oil into a large skillet ¼ inch deep, on medium heat, heat until oil sizzles.

Dip a tomato slice in egg mixture, coat with cornmeal mixture. Do not crowd in skillet. Fry tomatoes until golden, about 2 minutes per side. Transfer to a paper-towel lined plate to drain.

Build sandwich: Using hearty bread, toast and spread with mayonnaise. Add 2 Fried Green Tomato slices, at least 3 slices crisp bacon, and lettuce. Cut in half, serve with your favorite cole slaw; makes 4 servings.

A June Wedding in Kansas

I'm a romantic and love weddings. I have travelled to Kansas to attend the wedding of my nephew Steve and his beautiful wife-to-be, Kelli. When I first see Kelli walking towards her Groom, timeless elegance would describe her. Their wedding ceremony is full of charm, yet contemporary which seem to fit them both. A dinner reception followed with abundant food and a happy celebration while two families also came together and got to know each other. Their wedding day was special and perfect.

The following day the celebration continued as Kelli and Steve hosted a fun summer picnic/ barbecue on a lake for all their guests. It was a day of fun with boat rides, great food, and lots of laughing, all while the weather in Kansas cooperated.

Staying for several days, each evening found guests and family meeting at different restaurants for supper. That first night my sister-in-law Marge suggested crème brulee for dessert, which she and I shared. It was my first time trying it and I truly enjoyed everything about it and each night thereafter we shared a crème brulee; delicious, so light, and absolutely perfect with my after-dinner coffee.

Baking individual custards was very popular in the 1940's and 50's. The difference here is the sugar topping which is caramelized with a torch until it is crispy, called "burning the sugar".

Custard has been lifted to a new level.

VANILLA CRÈME BRULEE'

Makes six, 4ounce ramekins; Preheat oven to 325 degrees.

1. For the most intense vanilla flavor, pulverize 1/2 of a vanilla bean (chopped into ¼ inch pieces) with 2 tablespoons sugar to make "vanilla sugar". (A coffee grinder works great.) Note: May substitute vanilla bean with a tablespoon of pure vanilla extract (not imitation).

2. Warm 1 cup heavy cream, 1 cup half and half and vanilla sugar (if using) in a saucepan over medium heat just until steam rises.

3. In a mixing bowl whisk together 3 egg yolks, 1 egg, ¼ cup sugar, pinch of salt, and adding vanilla extract at this time if not using vanilla bean.

4. Temper hot cream mixture into eggs, strain into a measuring cup with a pour spout, and divide among six 4oz. ovenproof ramekins or custard cups. Arrange dishes in a baking pan, and then carefully transfer the pan to pre-heated oven. Add hot water to the pan and bake custards 35-45 minutes, or until just set; do not overcook.

Remove ramekins from the water bath, cool, then wrap loosely in plastic wrap in plastic wrap. Chill until completely cold, preferably overnight. The custards must be cold before caramelizing or they will melt.

Crème Brulee Sugar Topping -- Makes ¾ cup (for six 4oz. crème brulees)

Combine ½ cup brown sugar and ¼ cup white granulated sugar (raw sugar is good). Spread the mixture on a parchment-lined baking sheet. After baking the brulees, turn off the oven and place the baking sheet in the oven for an hour to dry out the sugar. Transfer to a food processor or coffee grinder to pulverize until fine Store in a tight container until ready to caramelize.

To caramelize top of brulee:

1. Blot custards dry with a paper towel. Sprinkle 1-2 tablespoons of sugar mixture over each.

2. Using a propane torch, melt sugar by waving flame 4-6 inches from surface. "Burn" until no dry sugar is visible.

Note: In regards to the torch, the consensus is that a small propane torch purchased at Wal-Mart, Target, or Home Depot for $20-$40 works well, apparently better than a butane torch.

Basics of crème brulee:
1. "Temper" the warm cream into the eggs, slowly whisking it in. Tempering raises the eggs' temperature without the risk of scrambling.

2. Setting them in a pan of water ensures the custard will not curdle. The sides of the pan should be no more than 2 inches high.

3. Bake the custards just until set. Test by tapping one, if it is still runny, bake 3to5 minutes more than test again. When they quiver like jello they are done.

CHAPTER 5
ALL ABOUT THE COOKS AND FOOD CHAT

A salute to the home cooks and foodies that became devoted readers and fans of my newspaper columns, *Cooking with Patricia* and *Pat's Kitchen.* The recipes in this chapter are from the personal collections of these cooks, sent to me to share with others.

There are also short stories which tell of my search to find lost recipes from their past. The first *lost recipe request* came from a veteran of the Korean War era who asked if I could locate or create a recipe for a dish he was served frequently in Stuttgart, Germany. The search became the story, and readers enjoyed following along.

Then there is Zena looking for a red bean dip recipe from a local restaurant of 50 years ago, and Alan, coming from FL to his 50th HS reunion, looking for tomato sausage from a long-ago market he and his mother would frequent. There are several of these poignant human interest stories, with found recipes, that may trigger a lost food memory of your own.

RECIPE DISCLAIMER

I, author, have not tested each recipe in this chapter and I assume no obligation or liability and make no warranties with respect to the recipes here. These "best" recipes were sent to me to share with others that want to try "good" recipes. May I add that when recipes are shared with others writing cookbooks, people usually send their "best" recipes with pride.

The recipes I have tested and made often I have designated with a star.

FINDING LOST RECIPES

PASTA CARBONARA

*GREEK LAMB & GREEN BEANS

JOSEPHINE'S SHRIMP ROSSINI

SUNDRIED TOMATO SAUSAGES

FAMOUS ANTIPASTO SUPREME WITH SHRIMP

A STORY; ZENA, ARTHUR, AND SEARCH FOR RED KIDNEY BEAN DIP

ITALIAN DODO'S

SHARING FAVORITE RECIPES

*APPLE WALNUT PIE; COURTESY SUE M, PELHAM NH

*PAUL'S PUMPKIN BARS AND FRIED ZUCCHINI CHIPS

LEMON LUSH

*CURRY-HONEY CHICKEN

*RHUBARB CRUNCH

AUSTRALIAN LAMINGTON

BLUEBERRY CAKE (50 YEAR OLD)

BEST EVER BANANA BREAD

DEDE'S TOURTIERE (FRENCH CANADIAN PORK PIE)

WATERGATE CAKE

*CHICKEN IN WHITE WINE SAUCE, COURTESY ANITA

*NEWBURYPORT RICE SALAD

FINDING LOST RECIPES

A VETERAN, ITALIAN PASTA, AND A MEMORY:

I received a note from Dean asking if I could find a recipe from his past, describing a pasta dish with no tomatoes, remembering eggs and possibly ham. Dean fondly remembered having this dish often at the Officer's Club at Patch Barracks, Stuttgart-Germany, assigned there from 1973-1976. After speaking to Dean seeking more clues, and searching through older Italian cookbooks, it appeared that what Dean had was Pasta Carbonara, a very traditional Italian recipe that was popular in the 1970's, he agreed and I sent him four versions of Pasta Carbonara. He called me a few weeks later happy that one of the four recipes I sent was very, very close saying he ate every" spec" of it, enjoying quite a fill. Dean further stated that at Stuttgart it was served good and hot, with extra cheese and crisp bacon at the table. Quoting Dean, "I loved that stuff, and couldn't get enough of it". When out of the service, he tried for years to duplicate it but never got it right. Dean concurs that the recipe below is as right as we're going to get it, unless we could find the Chef (possibly Italian) who made it at Patch Barracks. I laughed.

PASTA CARBONARA

INGREDIENTS: *8 ounces linguini or spaghetti*
4 eggs, beaten
1/3 cup half & half or light cream
1 cup grated parmesan cheese
1 cup pancetta (Italian bacon) or thick-cut bacon, cooked crisp and crumbled
1/4 cup chopped fresh parsley

Fresh ground black pepper to taste
Cook pasta according to package directions, drain
Beat eggs with cream and black pepper.

Cook pancetta over medium heat till crisp. (If it looks like there is too much fat from the bacon, pour some off)
Add pasta to the pancetta in fry pan, keeping hot. Pour cream/egg mixture in slowly, stirring continuously over medium heat for a couple of minutes (eggs get completely cooked with the hot pasta).
Add parsley and ¾ cup of the parmesan cheese and toss to coat well. Stir for 2-3 minutes and serve as Dean remembers it; good and hot, with bowls of grated cheese and crisp bacon on the table.

JOANNE T. RECALLS ITALIAN FOOD AND LAMB RECIPE ENJOYED IN BOSTON 1951-52

Joanne's e-mail:

"In the early 1950's I dined frequently at a small Italian restaurant on Stuart Street in Boston, Massachusetts. I have never had Italian food since to equal it, and I am a lover of Italian food. Would you be able to find the restaurant's name? Maybe there are descendants that still have a restaurant.

I also enjoyed eating at a Greek restaurant further up Tremont Street toward Egleston Square street-car-stop, actually a side street off Tremont. They served the most delicious Lamb with potatoes and string beans in a tomato sauce, it was to die for. I have never had it since. I would love to enjoy these foods again and would be grateful for your help." *Joanne T, Methuen*

I called Joanne to let her know I found three Italian restaurants on

Stuart Street, all having changed owners too many times over the years to help us solve that question.

However, I let Joanne know the lamb dish she is looking for is called "Arni me Fassolakia" (pronounced ahr-NEE-meh fah-soh-LAHK-yah); **Lamb and Green Beans.** This is a popular casserole cooked on top of the stove, with bone-in lamb preferred, stewed with tomatoes, potatoes, and string beans, seasoned deliciously with mint, cinnamon, and dill.

I have Lebanese friends who gave me their recipe for Lamb and Green beans several years ago and it is the same except for changes in the seasoning, no dill, using ground cloves and allspice instead.

LAMB & GREEN BEANS

INGREDIENTS: *4 pounds lamb, cut into large pieces (shoulder chops best)*

1 onion, chopped

½ cup olive oil

1 and ½ cups water

2 teaspoons kosher salt

2 and ¼ pounds fresh or frozen string beans (cut is best)

3 large tomatoes, peeled and pulped in blender

4 tablespoons tomato sauce

2 and ¼ pounds potatoes, peeled and cut into very large pieces

½ tablespoon chopped fresh mint

1 heaping tablespoon chopped fresh parsley

1/8 teaspoon ground cinnamon

1 heaping tablespoon chopped fresh dill

In a large pot on top of the stove, sauté the onion in olive oil, adding meat and cooking over medium heat until well browned. Add water, tomatoes, sauce, and 1 teaspoon of salt. Bring to a boil, cover and simmer for about 1 hour until meat is tender. Add beans, potatoes, and remaining seasonings. Bring to a boil, cover and simmer again for about 45 minutes. Add water if necessary, but this should be thick like a stew. Let sit off heat for 15 minutes before serving, great served on rice pilaf or plain rice, serves 4-6.

Update from Joanne T. – *"Finally had time to do some cooking and made the Greek lamb and bean dish, Bingo! I waited 56 years for that recipe, it was delicious. I can't wait for native green beans to be ready. By the way this is what my son had to say about the Greek dish, "Wow Ma, this is good! I think you're trying to keep me around with all these gourmet dishes." Then he had a second helping. Joanne T. Methuen MA*

Joanne T. also wrote that she loves a pasta dish she ate at Bertucci's restaurant and wanted to re-create it at home and could I get the recipe. She remembered it had a tomato sauce, shrimp, scallops, and capers served with Linguine. I called Bertucci's and they put me in touch with the corporate office. A gentleman stated their policy is not to give out tomato sauce and cream sauce recipes as they are secret. He could however, confirm that the dish was called "Shrimp Rossini" and at one time was served with scallops, but no longer.

Another reader saw Joanne's request and my reply in the paper. I received this e-mail from:

Josephine:

"Dear Pat, I love to cook. I came from Sicily in 1954 and have cooked since my teens, learning from my mother. I am able to re-create other dishes just from tasting them. I can help Joanne T. with the Bertucci dish, Shrimp Rossini, as I have made it before. Call on me anytime, you or others. I am 74 years old and the oldest of five sisters. I make many dishes that I never see in restaurants, as I love to cook, even Chinese dishes.

By the taste, I have figured the recipe ingredients for two people:"
Josephine

JOSEPHINE'S SHRIMP ROSSINI FOR TWO

INGREDIENTS: *½ pound linguine, cooked al dente*
4 tablespoons olive oil
1-2 fresh mushrooms, sliced
2 cups fresh or frozen broccoli flowerets
2 cloves garlic, chopped
1 pound shrimps
½ stick butter
1 fresh tomato, chopped OR ½ cup tomato sauce
1 cup light cream
1 cup of pasta water (from pot of cooked pasta)

Cook pasta. In a large skillet, heat oil and sauté defrosted broccoli and sliced mushrooms until tender, add butter and garlic with the shrimps and tomato and cook until shrimps turn pink (scallops can be added here if desired), cooking until scallops soft. When done, add cream, water and cooked pasta and toss until well coated. Serve with grated Romano cheese.

I was pleased to put Josephine in touch with Joanne T. a great combination of an experienced Italian cook and a lover of Italian food. These were two cooks who had a lot in common and a lot to talk about. *Pat*

FL to MA, 50th High School Reunion and Tomato Sausage

Letter from Alan,

"Dear Pat,

In September I will be traveling to Andover Massachusetts to attend my fiftieth Andover High School Reunion.
I have lived in Florida since finishing high school.
As a child growing up in Andover my mother frequently cooked tomato sausages. I have learned it is unique to that area, and requested it every time I got home. My Mother, and later my sisters, would prepare it, knowing it was a favorite. It was served either baked or pan-fried, along with mashed potato topped with delicious pan drippings. I really miss this dish, which I have found to be a New England treat (along with fish chowder, lobster, steamers, Indian pudding, and Moxie).

Pat, I just know that tomato sausage will not be on the reunion's menu, so I'll be looking in the area for a "tomato-sausage fix". The last time I was in the Merrimack Valley area was years ago, I found it in once, but it was made only one day a week and they were sold out, and I can't remember the name of that place.

Could you help me with this nostalgic culinary memory? Would you know the origin? I have heard French-Canadian and Italian." *Alan N. Miami, Florida*

My Response to Alan,

I made some calls, and found a few stores in the Lawrence-Methuen-Salem New Hampshire area that still make their own sausages. As far as origin, I believe many cultures made their own sausage; most definitely Italian, Portuguese, and Polish.

I spoke with Kenny from THWAITE'S MKT, on Railroad Street in Methuen Massachusetts. He was very helpful and told me that yes; they still made tomato sausage, now for six generations. Their recipe is a secret one handed down from his great-grandmother. The recipe originated in England, her being English. Kenny believes that the tomato sausages may have first became popular in this area in the 1920's at his Great-grandmother's boarding house, which is what led to her opening the present store on Railroad Street in the later 1920's, and is still going strong today, especially the hugely popular tomato sausages and English pork pies.

Alan, if you stop in to Thwaite's market you will get your tomato sausage. Who knows, this might be the very place you and your Mother came to in your childhood. Welcome back to the area and enjoy your reunion. Cordially, *Pat*

SUN-DRIED TOMATO SAUSAGE (NOT THWAITES MARKET SECRET RECIPE)

INGREDIENTS: *5 pounds ground pork*
¾ pound whole milk mozzarella, cut into ¼ inch cubes
1 bunch Italian parsley, finely chopped
6 ½ ounce sun-dried tomatoes in oil, coarsely chopped
1 tablespoon of each: dried basil, fennel seed, coarse black pepper, salt, ground coriander
¾ cup dry white wine

Blend seasonings with wine. Mix seasoning mixture with ground meat and cubed cheese, stuff mixture into casings.

A Mother's Food Memory; Salad Made Famous at Mama Leone's in New York

We all have memories of food. Sometimes these can be childhood memories that are often triggered by a scent or taste, possibly the aroma of baking bread or lamb roasting that is spiced with Syrian pepper. Many of these memories are connected to holidays, but not always. I have had several readers write to me regarding a food memory that they would like to bring alive again.

This past week I received a very interesting note from a gentleman in Michigan who wanted to find a recipe for a salad made famous by Mama Leone's restaurant in New York. Following is Dennis's note which will explain his request, and how I became involved. I might add that I love the challenge and pleasure I get from the search, which always leads to interesting places, people, and circumstances that just fascinate me. It is amazing what comes out of the woodwork when I help someone find a lost recipe. I love what comes from it.

"Hello Ms. Altomare.

When searching on the internet, I found you from a newspaper article you wrote last year about the famous Mama Leone's restaurant. Unfortunately I never did dine there, but I believe my parents have. I wonder if you would, by chance, have the recipe for their famous salad. My mother used to make it back in the late 1950's. I have raved about it to my wife, as did my Mother, as a wonderful salad that she has missed out on. My best recollection of the ingredients is radishes, anchovy, endive, lettuce and tomato, but it is a faint memory. I'll cross my fingers that this might be enough to solve this mystery. I grew up in Wash D.C in the 1950's/60's. Neither my Mother nor I can remember how to make it.

Might you have the recipe? If not, where I could find it? I have looked all over the internet.

Many thanks."   Dennis K, Michigan

I replied to Dennis's note explaining that I have a copy of the cookbook that Mama Leone's son, Gene Leone, wrote in 1967 containing his mother's recipes from her personal kitchen and her famous restaurant. In the salad section was written this paragraph:

"Created by her in her modest small kitchen in her own home, while dreaming of one day when she would open her own little restaurant, Mother's antipasto with shrimps and her special sauce, became the toast of connoisseurs, world-famed celebrities and literally millions of friends and diners who graced Leone's Restaurant during the past half century." *Son, Gene Leone*

It appears the antipasto with shrimp may be the famous salad that Dennis's mother used to enjoy back in the 1950's. Out of all the recipes in the cookbook, Gene Leone speaks of the fame of Mama Leone's antipasto.

We should treat ourselves and make this anytime for our families and friends, and enjoy an obviously great Italian shrimp antipasto.

MAMA LEONE'S ANTIPASTO SUPREME WITH SHRIMP

Serves 4

INGREDIENTS: *6 slices Italian salami, ¼ inch thick*
                        1 large green, red or yellow pepper
                        16-18 jumbo shrimps, cooked
                        2 celery stalks with leaves, diced

6 whole fresh green scallions, diced
3 hard-cooked eggs, quartered
3 medium-size hard tomatoes, quartered
pinch salt – pinch freshly ground black pepper
6 heaping tablespoons Shrimp sauce (recipe follows)

Cut salami into strips 1 ¼ inches long, and slice peppers into long thin strips. Place in a large bowl with shrimps, diced celery and scallions; refrigerate. Refrigerate eggs and tomatoes separately. When ready to serve, add salt and pepper to shrimp mixture and toss. Serve on a bed of endive and greens that have been dotted with a few anchovy's. Arrange eggs and tomatoes over top. Spoon shrimp sauce over all.

Shrimp Sauce: A simple but delicious sauce, always homemade by Mrs. Leone or her staff.

Makes about 2 cups

INGREDIENTS: *2 whole green scallions or 1 tablespoon grated sweet*
onion
6 tablespoons finely chopped fresh green or red pepper
2 tablespoons Spanish capers, chopped fine
2 tablespoons prepared horse-radish
1 cup mayonnaise, regular or light
½ cup chili sauce
½ teaspoon crushed red pepper
½ teaspoon freshly ground black pepper
½ teaspoon salt
1 garlic clove, mashed

Slice scallions lengthwise and chop fine, or grate the sweet onion. Place scallions or onion, green or red pepper, capers and horseradish in a strainer and drain for 15 minutes. Combine mayonnaise and chili sauce in a bowl. Add red and black pepper, salt and garlic. Whip together with a whisk. Add drained ingredients and beat or mix well. Taste for salt. Refrigerate. Use over shrimps, crabmeat, or cold lobster.

Leone's Italian Cookbook was published in 1967 and written by her son Gene Leone.

I wrote a column on this book as it is a treasure trove of fascinating information, such as best wine to compliment a dish, cooking equipment to have on hand, and a very interesting Foreword written by President Dwight Eisenhower dated 1966. A few tidbits of information: Mama Leone's opened in 1906 with only 20 seats. Enrico Caruso sang at her opening. The restaurant became one of the most legendary Italian restaurants in our country, with many trying to reproduce her recipes. The restaurant grew to 1500 seats by the 1930's, serving up to 6000 dinners nightly. Sadly, after Mama Leone's death, the restaurant was sold in 1939.

Following is a hand-written note I received regarding Mama Leone's cookbook:

"Dear Pat, My name is Isabelle. I read your write-up about Mama Leone's and would like to offer you my copy of Leone's Italian Cookbook;
It's clean and in good shape, although like me it shows its age. I have had it a long time but have no-one to give it to. I could give it somewhere, but I'd rather not. I celebrate my 95th birthday this year and what cooking I do, and I do cook, is out of my head. Please give me a call." *Isabelle, Hampstead New Hampshire*

I contacted Isabelle right away and enjoyed chatting about cookbooks, cooking and her family. I was very pleased to accept her offer and added her copy of Mama Leone's cookbook to my collection. It is special to me though, as inside the front cover I have taped a copy of Isabelle's r note; it is a reminder of the memories we all treasure that are centered on our families and our kitchens.

For reasons only she knows this cookbook was important to Isabelle; I will certainly take care of it.

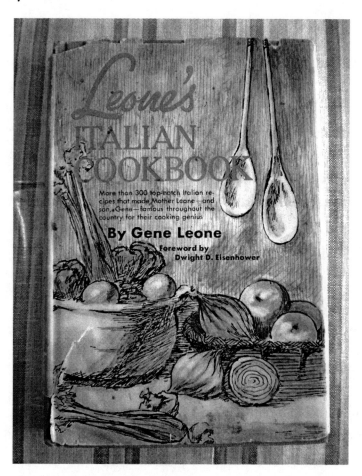

MEMORIES SPARKED BY LONG-AGO RESTAURANT

Ann Gebala excitedly sent me a note about her life in New York City in her twenties.

She read about Mama Leone's restaurant which she hadn't thought about in more than fifty years. In her 80's now, she had so much to share. We made a date for tea. Ann was very interesting to talk with, and her memory was clear and vast. When she read about Mama Leone's restaurant, it brought back memories of her living and working in New York City.

Antoinette Gebala, called Ann, stated her family moved from Methuen Massachusetts to the East Side of New York when she was two years old. When she was a young woman, she and her sisters worked at Knickerbockers Toy Company on Sixth Street. There were other Italian girls there and soon she had made many friends. "The Italian girls", as she refers to her group, would go to lunch together and one of their favorite places to eat was Mama Leone's restaurant, close by in the Theatre district. She spoke of the fun and camaraderie of those lunch times at Mama Leone's, and of the great food they enjoyed, one of her favorites the Antipasto special.

One of Ann's clear memories of her working life was when Mrs. Roosevelt came to the toy store to shop. This is only one of so many fascinating tidbits of her "New York City Life".

Ann returned to Methuen in 1947, met her husband and was soon married. She is proud of her Italian heritage, but has very much embraced her husband's Polish heritage. Ann and a friend love Polish dancing, and when they can find one, like to attend the Polish club's old-fashioned picnics.

By her own admission, she is not a very good cook, but loves Polish food as much as Italian, loves cookbooks and finding good recipes, and is thankful her daughter has become such a good cook.

(Antoinette Gebala's full name is printed with her permission).

ZENA, ARTHUR AND RED KIDNEY BEAN DIP

I received a hand-written note from Zena of Lawrence, Massachusetts. She was looking for the recipe for Red Kidney Bean Dip she first had in the 1970's at a restaurant called Arthur's Town House, off Essex Street in Lawrence. She stated she enjoyed this thick and chunky dip often at the restaurant and would love to get his recipe so she could make it again.

I wrote Zena that I had checked the internet and a 2006 Lawrence telephone directory and it appeared that Arthur's restaurant was replaced by the "Townhouse Pub" on Newbury Street which is very close to Essex and Jackson streets. The telephone number listed for the Pub was out of service. I did locate two different versions of red kidney bean dip and mailed them to Zena, hoping one would be close to her memory.

A week later I received this e-mail:

"Dear Patricia, My name is John D., son of Arthur, who owned Arthur's Town House in Lawrence. I saw your article of Zena looking for my Dad's bean dip recipe. My father would be happy to pass it on to her. He is not computer savvy but you can call him, he's looking forward to hearing from you. He is so excited that someone from 43 years ago remembers his bean dip and the restaurant."

After contacting John, Arthur, and Zena, and passing around telephone numbers, Zena and Arthur first connected by phone, and as of writing this, have gotten together to share the recipe and talk of old times at the restaurant and in Lawrence. It took Arthur a few days to recall all the ingredients of his dip; he never did have a written recipe. Arthur does remember how he came about to make it, which was when someone gave him large #10 cans of kidney beans and he needed to find a way to use them. He would rinse and drain the beans, mash them only slightly and mix with mayonnaise, red relish, and green relish for color, horse-radish, pinch of basil, vinegar, onion, and celery salt or finely chopped celery, most probably adding ingredients to taste.

I can't think of a better cooking complement than someone remembering forty-three years later how good a recipe was.

Responses received:

Dear Patricia,

I would love to have the recipe mentioned in your newspaper article for a red bean dip from Arthur's Town House restaurant, which used to be in Lawrence many years ago. I loved reading the story about it.
Thank you, Patricia in Methuen

I love red bean dip and was hoping by the end of the article you would list it. Please forward me a copy of Arthur's Town House Bean Dip. I enjoyed following Zena and Arthur's story.   **_Jean_**

Several local cooks are quick to find Linda's Traditional Christmas cookie

Linda A. wrote that she loved a cookie she called "chocolate todos" since childhood, a Christmas tradition in her home. She explained she had lost her recipe and hadn't made them for two years. I put a short blurb in the paper asking cooks out there if they could help Linda. I received four versions for the cookies, each named slightly different; Italian Dodos, toe toe cookies, tho tho's, and chocolate todos.

The recipes I received differed only in spice amounts, all were frosted and contained nuts. I learned that Todo's are an Italian chocolate-cinnamon spice cookie. Some folk's frost, others do not. Readers *D.B.* and *Cucina* responded that their family does not frost. Several people were adamant that Christmas Cookie baking is not complete without Todo's, and others wanted the recipes so they could try them.

Comment from *Mary L.: I have been making Italian Toto (her spelling) cookies for over thirty years when a then co-worker shared her recipe with me and Christmas cookie making isn't done until I make delicious toto's.*

I was pleased to provide Linda and others with the recipes I received, and no matter what they are called I am anxious to make Todo's myself.

Joyce H. of Methuen Massachusetts sent me this version, called Dodos, which she states is a family favorite that she has made for many years. Quoting Joyce *"this may differ slightly from the taste Linda is used to, but I promise she will be pleasantly surprised with the flavor. I'm sure she will be serving these cookies for many holidays to come"*.

ITALIAN DODOS

INGREDIENTS: *4 and ½ cups sifted flour*
½ cup cocoa
1 teaspoon ground cloves
1 teaspoon ground cinnamon
1 tablespoon baking powder
1 cup sugar
2 eggs
1 teaspoon vanilla
1 teaspoon orange extract
¾ cup warm milk
¾ cup melted shortening
1 cup finely chopped walnuts

Mix dry ingredients and set aside. In a larger bowl beat eggs, sugar, and flavorings. Add dry ingredients to egg mixture. Add milk and cooled melted shortening, mixing until well blended. Add nuts and mix with hands if necessary to blend in. Form dough into small balls size of a walnut. Place on ungreased cookie sheet. Bake at 375 degrees for 12 to 15 minutes. Important to not overcook, test at 10 minutes as ovens vary.

FROSTING:
1 pound confectioners' sugar, sifted
3 tablespoons cocoa, sifted
10 tablespoons milk
¼ teaspoon cinnamon
½ teaspoon vanilla

Frosting is better if not too thin; spread a thick coating on top of each cookie.

SHARING FAVORITE RECIPES

Recipes in this section were sent to me by home cooks who wanted to share their best family recipes with others who also enjoy cooking for their family and friends, sharing recipes, and chatting about all of it.

FAMILY FAVORITE RECIPE FROM SUE

"I found this recipe about four years ago in a women's magazine, and have been making it ever since, my family loves it. I'm always getting requests for the recipe, so now I have it on my computer so I have a quick copy, of which I am forwarding to you. The recipe caught my eye because of the ground walnut layer in the bottom of the pie. When you take a bite you get the buttery walnuts with the apples. I always make two, because if I don't I might not get a piece. Once when my daughter Missy made it she

accidentally put in an extra tablespoon of butter in the walnut mixture. It was so good that I do it every time now." Sue M. Pelham New Hampshire

Apple Walnut Pie

Makes a 9 inch pie

Need Pastry for 2 crust pie; your own recipe or pre-made (found in refrigerated section of market)

BOTTOM LAYER: *¾ Cup ground walnuts*
2 tablespoons brown sugar
2 tablespoons beaten egg
1 tablespoon milk
2 to 3 tablespoons soft butter
¼ teaspoon vanilla extract
Sprinkle of lemon juice

FILLING: *5 -6 cups peeled, sliced apples*
1 tablespoon lemon juice
¾ cup sugar
2 tablespoons flour
1 teaspoon cinnamon
¼ teaspoon nutmeg
¼ teaspoon salt
2 tablespoons softened butter

In a bowl combine walnuts, brown sugar, egg, milk, 2-3 tablespoons butter, vanilla and lemon juice. Place this mixture on top of the bottom pastry and smooth evenly.

In large bowl, toss apples with lemon juice. Combine sugar, flour, cinnamon, nutmeg and salt. Toss with apples; spoon on nut mixture, dot with 2 tablespoons butter.

Place top crust over apples. Bake at 375 degrees for 50 – 60 minutes until golden brown.

Celebrating Autumn with Pumpkin Bars

Since it is autumn, I thought I'd share one of my favorite pumpkin recipes with you (I love pumpkin in any way, shape or form!). Years ago I found this recipe in a magazine and have shared it with several friends.
Pat B. Andover Massachusetts

Paul's Pumpkin Bars

INGREDIENTS: *4 eggs*
1 and 2/3 cups granulated sugar
1 cup cooking oil
1 (16ounce) can pumpkin
2 cups all purpose flour
2 teaspoons baking powder
2 teaspoons ground cinnamon
1 teaspoon salt
1 teaspoon baking soda

In mixer bowl, beat together eggs, granulated sugar, oil and pumpkin until light and fluffy. Stir together flour, baking powder, cinnamon, salt, and soda. Add to pumpkin mixture and mix thoroughly. Spread batter in ungreased 15x10 inch baking pan. Bake 350 degrees for 25 to 30 minutes. Cool.

CREAM CHEESE ICING: *1 (3 ounce) package cream cheese, softened*
½ cup butter or margarine, softened
1 teaspoon vanilla extract
2 cups sifted powdered sugar

Cream together cream cheese and butter, stir in vanilla. Add powdered sugar, a little at a time, and beat well until mixture is smooth. Frost with Cream Cheese Icing, cut into 24 bars.

Note: I discovered that my Mom's recipe for pumpkin bars is the same as Pat B's. I can attest to their moistness and mild pumpkin flavor. You will not be disappointed. Raisins optional.

Pat B. also sent this delightful frosting recipe and following is a different way to try zucchini:

"Here is my all-time favorite, easy, go-to frosting recipe I have use for years: 1 cup milk, ½ pint heavy cream, and one small package instant pudding. This frosts a two-layer cake or one sheet cake. Combine any flavor cake mix with a flavor pudding (in the frosting) that you like. My daughter's favorite is white cake and vanilla frosting, decorated with strawberries".

"Easy and delicious; no matter how many I make, there are never any leftovers!" Pat B.

Fried Zucchini Chips

Cut 2 or 3 zucchinis in quarter inch rounds. Toss them in extra virgin olive oil. Mix ¼ cup seasoned bread crumbs with ¼ cup grated parmesan cheese. Add salt & pepper.
Press zucchini rounds into the crumb mixture and place on a greased cookie sheet.

Bake approximately 15 minutes in a pre-heated 450 degree oven, just until slightly browned.

Always looking for more recipes to use zucchini in the Fall, Sharon sent me two of her favorites with her note:

"Hi Pat, You have been so helpful to me through your column I wanted to share these recipes with you. I receive many requests for the casserole for cookouts and pot luck dinners. My nephew adds cooked chicken, makes a salad and he has a meal. The relish I have been making for years; got away from it when working, now retired and I find it rewarding and enjoyable again." Roger and Sharon, Methuen Massachusetts

ZUCCHINI CASSEROLE

INGREDIENTS: *6 cups zucchini*
¼ cup chopped onion
1 can cream of mushroom soup
1 cup sour cream
1cup shredded carrot
8 ounce package dry stuffing mix such as Pepperidge Farm brand
½ cup butter, melted

Cook squash and onion in boiling water for 5 minutes. Drain well. Mix soup and sour cream together and stir in shredded carrot. Fold in squash and onion mixture. In separate dish or pan, mix melted butter and stuffing mix. Spread half of stuffing mix on bottom of 9" x 13" casserole dish. Cover with vegetable mixture and top with remaining stuffing mixture. Bake at 350degrees for 30 minutes.

Note from Pat: My mother had this same recipe in her collection; I believe it was very popular in the 1970's-80's.

ZUCCHINI RELISH

INGREDIENTS: *12 cups coarsely ground zucchini, unpeeled*
5 medium onions
1 green bell pepper
1 red bell pepper
5 tablespoons salt
3 cups sugar
2 and 1/2 cups cider vinegar
2 tablespoons cornstarch
1 teaspoon mustard seed
1 teaspoon turmeric
2 tablespoons celery seeds

Coarsely grind onions and peppers. Stir in zucchini and salt. Cover and allow to sit for 3 hours. Drain and rinse well. Combine the remaining ingredients to make a syrup, boiling until sugar dissolves and mixture has thickened. Add to vegetables and cook for 20 minutes.
Ladle into hot canning jars, adjust seals; process in a boiling water bath for 10 minutes.

A SIMPLY YUMMY DESSERT

Cathy D. recommends this dessert for springtime, saying it is light and refreshing. Quick and easy to prepare, Cathy tells me it was given to her by a friend where she works, and describes it as simply "very yummy".

Lemon Lush
INGREDIENTS:
CRUST: *1 stick cold butter (Use salted butter or add scant ¼ teaspoon salt with flour.)*
1 and 1/2 cups of flour

Mix flour and butter until crumbly. Spray bottom of 9"x13" pan with cooking spray (non-stick pan recommended)
Press into bottom of pan. Bake at 350 degrees until light brown, 15-20 minutes.

1ST LAYER   *2 (8 ounce) packages cream cheese*
2 cups powdered sugar
1 (8 ounce) tub whipped topping (such as Cool Whip brand)

Mix cream cheese and powdered sugar till blended. Add whipped topping and stir till blended.
Spread on cooled crust.

2ND LAYER   *Mix 3 packages of instant lemon pudding with 4 and 1/2 cups of milk. Spread onto cream cheese layer.*

TOP LAYER   *Spread 2nd (8 ounce) tub of whipped topping. Garnish with walnut halves, blueberries, or lemon zest.*

My additional note: This makes a good amount and would be great to take to a cookout or family get-together, as long as it could be kept refrigerated.

From Stan, "Best Thing I Cook"

"Here is a recipe that is the best thing I cook. I can't say I'm a great cook, but there are some things I make often enough to have them come out

right. This always comes out good, so I know other people will like it. I'm a single guy and have locked onto your column now and learned a few good things." Stan, No. Andover Massachusetts

CURRY-HONEY CHICKEN

INGREDIENTS: *8 chicken thighs*
¾ cup honey
¼ cup Dijon mustard
2 teaspoons curry powder
2 teaspoons salt

Place chicken skin side up in a lightly greased 9x13 baking dish. Combine remaining ingredients; spread over chicken. Bake uncovered at 375 degrees for 45 minutes, basting a few times. Serves 6-8

FAVORITE RHUBARB RECIPE

Alyce's suggestions when making this: Serve warm with vanilla ice cream and double the recipe for a get-together.

RHUBARB CRUNCH DESSERT

Preheat oven to 350 degrees.

BASE: COMBINE: *1 cup flour*
5 tablespoons confectioners' sugar
½ cup melted butter or margarine (use salted butter)
Press into a 9 inch pan. Bake 15 minutes.
FILLING: *2 eggs*
1 and ½ cups granulated sugar

¼ cup flour
¾ teaspoon baking powder
Pinch of salt
2 cups cut-up rhubarb

Beat eggs well, add sugar and mix until dissolved. Slowly add flour, baking powder, and salt. Mix in rhubarb till mixture well blended. Pour on crust. Bake again for 35 to 45 minutes. (At least 45 minutes if recipe is doubled).

Serve warm or cold. Good with vanilla ice cream (especially if warm), or whipped topping.

Note from Pat: When I made this for a Memorial Day cookout it was a big hit with a great tasting "custardy" filling that compliments the rhubarb.

You Will be Surprised What a Lamington is!

It is a small cake cube that has been dipped in chocolate icing, then rolled in desiccated coconut. A mainstay in Australia commonly found at fairs, school functions, and bake sales around the country, much like our brownies and chocolate chip cookies.
In 2006, the Lamington was inducted into the National Trust of Heritage Icons. Since then each year on July 21, Australians celebrate "National Lamington Day".
How was the Lamington brought to my attention? **Barbara, living in Queensland Australia,** contacted **me via e-mail,** explaining that her brother in New Hampshire had been sending her my recipes he clipped from the newspaper. Barbara e-mailed me several times and I found her

life in Australia very interesting. She teaches, raises Dexter beef cattle, and is involved in her local church activities.

At my request for an authentic recipe from her country, she sent me this Lamington recipe and told me about herself.

Barbara moved to Australia in 1970 with her two children and American husband. Her first invitation to a "come for morning coffee" with a few of the wives was welcoming, but being a "new Australian" she wanted to do the right thing, so asked what she could bring. "Oh just a few pikelets or lamingtons would be nice", was suggested. She exclaimed "say what?" wondering what those were. Barbara learned that Pikelets are tiny pancakes, similar to crepes, served with jam and whipped cream.

Barbara selected this recipe for Lamingtons from a popular 1979 cookbook for school students, "Everyday Cookery", written by a Home Economics teacher.

Australian Lamingtons

Makes 16 individual cake squares

INGREDIENTS:
CAKE:

3 eggs
½ cup superfine sugar (called castor sugar in Australia)
¾ cup self-rising flour
¼ cup cornstarch (called corn flour in Australia)
3 teaspoons butter
3 tablespoons hot water

Beat eggs together until light and fluffy. Gradually add sugar and continue beating until mixture is thick and sugar completely dissolved. Sift dry ingredients together 3 times. Melt butter in hot water. Lightly fold dry ingredients into egg mixture. Fold in butter and water mixture quickly. Pour into a greased 7" x10 ½ " shallow baking pan. Bake in moderate oven, 350 degrees for 30 minutes or when toothpick inserted comes out clean.

CHOCOLATE ICING: *1 pound confectioners' sugar*
1/3 cup cocoa
3 teaspoons soft butter
½ cup milk

Sift confectioners' sugar and cocoa into a bowl or top half of a double boiler. Add soft butter and milk. Stir with a wooden spoon and mix thoroughly. Stand over hot water stirring constantly until icing is of good coating consistency.

Trim cake, cut into 16, 2 inch cubes. Hold each cake on a fork and dip edges into the chocolate icing until coated. Drain off excess. Put cakes individually into a bowl of coconut* coating evenly. Let stand on a wire rack until completely dry.

*10 ounces or ¾ pound desiccated coconut (Coconut that is dried longer to remove more moisture content. It is widely used by bakers and pastry chefs. If you are unable to find it, use regular dried coconut)

A Reader's comment;

"I was so interested in reading about the lamingtons. My son just got back from Australia and I saved it for him to read. He said you were right that these little cakes are popular. He is not a sweets lover so he didn't have any, but says everyone eats them. I love sweets so I am going to make them some time as they sound delicious". Jeannie, Groveland

BLUEBERRY CAKE WITH A HISTORY

Joan loves blueberries, and wanted to share her favorite way of using them in her baking; a cake recipe she has had for over fifty years. She states she got it from a neighbor, who had it when she was a child. Joan has made this cake for all these years and says everyone who tries it loves it.

BLUEBERRY CAKE

Preheat oven to 350 degrees

INGREDIENTS: *2 cups flour*
3 level teaspoons baking powder
1/3 level teaspoon salt
2 cups blueberries (fresh or frozen)
3/4 cup granulated sugar
1 egg
2 tablespoons melted shortening (Joan uses vegetable oil)
1 cup milk

Sift together flour, salt, baking powder. Add sugar and mix to a stiff batter with the egg, shortening, and milk. Add blueberries. Bake in a 9x13 greased pan, approximately 30 minutes. Top should be light golden brown.

_____

*"I am sending this recipe for **Best Ever Banana Bread**, made a little different with the addition of frozen wild blueberries. Best wishes for continued sharing with all of us" Jan, Methuen*

BEST EVER BANANA BREAD (OR MUFFINS)

Preheat oven to 325 degrees

INGREDIENTS: *1 ¾ cups all purpose flour*
1 ½ cups sugar
1 teaspoon baking soda
½ teaspoon salt
2 eggs
1 cup mashed ripe bananas, (2 to 3)
½ cup vegetable oil
¼ cup plus 1 tablespoon vanilla yogurt
1 teaspoon vanilla extract
1 cup chopped nuts (optional)
1 cup wild blueberries - frozen

In a large bowl stir flour, sugar, baking soda and salt. In another bowl combine eggs, bananas, oil, yogurt, and vanilla extract. Add to flour mixture, stirring just till moistened. Fold in nuts and blueberries. Pour into greased 9x5x3 inch loaf pan. Bake 1 hour plus 20 minutes or until toothpick inserted in center comes out dry.
For muffins bake 25 minutes or till tested dry.

DEDE'S CHRISTMAS TRADITION; FRENCH CANADIAN PORK PIE, "TOURTIERE" (PRONOUNCED TOOK-KAY)

Dede explains her family's customs:

"The French custom, as I remember from my childhood, was that tourtiere was served after attending midnight mass on Christmas Eve. The fasting rules for receiving communion at that time were very strict, leaving

a long time with nothing to eat or drink before one received communion at mass. By the time people got home, many hungry hours had passed.

We would leave our house around 11 p.m. in order to get a seat, because midnight mass was always packed to the rafters in most churches. Of course part of Christmas Eve night was arriving early to hear the choir sing beautiful Christmas carols before mass began, thus, «officially» starting Christmas Eve. Since High Mass said on Christmas Eve usually lasted anywhere from *one and a half to two hours (or more after all the Merry Christmases were said), we were pretty hungry by the time we arrived home.*

After returning from midnight mass, relatives would gather together at one home and there would be a feast of delicious foods. Several «took-kays» were always on the table prepared by different aunts and grandmothers. After eating all kinds of special holiday food, we would stay up and open our gifts, finally going to bed in the wee hours of the morning.

Today, since Christmas mass times are more frequent, many families choose to eat their "took-kay" in the morning for breakfast. This is the custom that my family has adopted. The aroma of the pie cooking in the oven early in the morning woke up the family in anticipation of starting a wonderful Christmas day. Others like to take a tourtiere along to a Christmas dinner. No matter when it was eaten, tourtiere was always part of the French tradition in celebrating Christmas.

Many French people serve tourtiere at Thanksgiving as well. Since pork is more plentiful now, many do not wait to serve it just on Thanksgiving and Christmas. It is a culinary favorite that can be enjoyed all winter long.

Hope you give it a try and become a French Canadian for one Christmas Eve! Ah oui!" Dede B. Hampstead New Hampshire

Tourtiere (French Canadian Pork Pie)

INGREDIENTS: *2 ½ pounds lean ground pork*
1 large onion, diced
½ teaspoon **each***; cinnamon, cloves, nutmeg*
1 ½ teaspoons salt
¼ teaspoon pepper
¼ teaspoon Bell's seasoning (or poultry seasoning)
2 cups water
1 large potato, peeled and boiled
Crust for (two) 9" pies (top and bottom)

Makes two good sized meat pies

In a large saucepan, combine ground pork, onion, cinnamon, cloves, nutmeg, salt and pepper. Brown meat and onions for about 5 minutes on medium/low heat; Cover meat mixture with 2 cups of water. Simmer on low heat for approximately 1 and one-half to 2 hours, until meat is light brown and water on the bottom of pan has almost completely evaporated. Stir occasionally. If water evaporates too quickly and meat is sticking to the bottom of the pan, add a little water, as necessary, to keep mixture moist during cooking time. When finished, there should be only about a tablespoon of water with juices remaining on the bottom.

While meat is cooking, boil potato until soft but not mushy. Drain and mash cooked potato with a fork, leaving tiny chunks for texture. Set aside.

When meat is done, stir in ¼ teaspoon of Bell's seasoning into meat mixture. Fold in mashed potato. Place half of the meat filling in one of the prepared 9" pie plates. Cover with the top crust. Make vent holes in top of crust. Repeat with the remaining meat and other pie crust. Bake at 350 degrees for approximately 40 minutes until top crust is golden brown. Bon appetite!

Dede's Note: Some people like to use ground pork butt, but I find that it makes the meat filling fatty and greasy. I prefer to use lean ground pork in my recipe, and the taste is not compromised.

WHO IS AUNTIE MIMO? WHAT IS CHATTERLINE? DAISY'S LETTER EXPLAINS;

Here is the lovely letter I received along with a recipe:

Dear Pat,

I saw the recipe for "Watergate Salad" in one of your columns. I had never seen that recipe, but have had the recipe for "Watergate Cake" for many years, and thought you and might like it. It brought back memories.

"Aunty Mimo" was a very much loved contributor to "chatterline" which was in the Boston Herald Newspaper way back when. I tried to never miss it. I have kept many of her recipes including this Watergate Cake. One day she announced that she had written a cookbook and it would be for sale for only a short time. I had a brief illness and forgot about the cookbook. When I was able to send in the money for it, it was too late, which really disappointed me. Whatever happened to her I will never know. I really wanted that cookbook as she had terrific recipes. I learned a lesson; if you want it bad enough, go after it. Sincerely, Daisy

Watergate Cake

INGREDIENTS: *1 lg. box cake mix, white or yellow*

1 small package pistachio instant pudding
1 cup vegetable oil
½ cup finely ground walnuts, pecans, or pistachios
3 large eggs
1 cup milk

In large mixing bowl, combine dry cake mix and dry pudding mix. Add eggs and blend well. Add oil, nuts and milk. Beat medium speed for 4 minutes. Pour into well greased 13x9 baking pan or a bundt pan.

Bake at 350 degrees for 45-50 minutes; (may be longer when in a bundt pan) Check for doneness.

FROSTING:

Combine 1 box instant pistachio pudding with an 8 ounce container of whipped topping, or 1 and one-quarter cups cold milk.
Decorate with green or red maraschino cherries, coconut, and halved pecans if desired. Coconut can be tinted green if making for St. Patrick's Day.

Soon after the Watergate Cake and Daisy's letter was in the newspaper I received several e-mails expressing interest in what now has become the **"Auntie Mimo" story**. "Arlene" wrote me that she was delighted to hear of another fan, exclaiming that Auntie Mimo's recipes were terrific. Arlene continued, saying she had lost most all the newspaper clippings of Auntie Mimo's recipes, especially her favorite "Spaghetti and Meatballs". Arlene specifically wanted to contact Daisy for copies.

After a lengthy internet search I was able to gain some clarity on Auntie Mimo and "chatterline." I found that Chatterline was indeed a popular column in the Boston Herald. Auntie Mimo was a frequent contributor and produced a cook-booklet that was available for purchase. I continued to search for Auntie Mimo and for some of her recipes and found a connection to Auntie Mimo through a *blog hosted by Anita, a fan of Gus Saunders & the Yankee Kitchen,* along with Auntie Mimo. I called Anita and told her of Daisy's letter and Arlene's response, as well as the interest surrounding Auntie Mimo. From Anita, I learned that the Yankee Kitchen was called the Boston Kitchen in its earlier days. Gus Saunders was the radio host who became very well known. Anita went on to say she did not have the Auntie Mimo cook-booklet, but believes that Auntie Mimo was a frequent contributor to other sources, Yankee Kitchen Cookbook and an old Boston Globe Cookbook from the 1970's, as well as to Chatterline, a Boston Herald column, and Confidential Chat in the Boston Globe.

Anita established her blog/site specifically to connect with former listeners and exchange recipes. She has a few of Auntie Mimo's recipes, as well as recipes from the Yankee Kitchen program, some posted on her blog. I have been on her site and any "foodie", or person interested in good recipes, will find it interesting.

Go to http://ykconnection.blogspot.com.

This recipe is not from the Yankee Kitchen but is a personal recipe of Anita's that she has developed over the years, and recently gave to me.

Anita tells us about her "tried and true" family recipe:

"I first made this recipe when I was in my 20s and dating my husband to-be. My mother and step-father were away at our cottage in Maine which meant that my boyfriend and I had the house to ourselves. Mike was out back, mowing the lawn, and I was in the kitchen preparing what would be our first dinner as a couple. When dinner was ready, I put on a dress and my mother's pearls, and stood by the back door trying to get his attention. I was going for a whole June Cleaver, "Leave it to Beaver" thing.

The original recipe called for veal and Madeira and was from <u>The Cookbook: Worcester Art Museum,</u> published in 1976. I've varied the recipe extensively using chicken instead of veal, white wine and no Madeira, and made a few other changes as well. The basic principle is the same, sautéing, then simmering in beef stock and wine, resulting in a beautiful sauce.

This dish is always a hit. What's more, it's the perfect party dish as it keeps exceptionally well on a buffet or on the stove."

CHICKEN IN WHITE WINE SAUCE

Recipe courtesy of Anita Bennett @ Yankee Kitchen Connection.com

INGREDIENTS: *2 pounds boneless chicken breast*
                    3 tablespoons olive oil
                    1/3 cup flour
                    1/3 cup finely grated parmesan cheese
                    ¼ teaspoon nutmeg
                    Salt & pepper
                    2 cloves garlic, peeled & sliced
                    1/2 cup beef stock
                    1 cup white wine
                    Lemon and parsley for garnish

Slice chicken into serving pieces. Between waxed paper, pound chicken to a quarter inch thickness. Mix flour, cheese, nutmeg, salt and pepper in a bowl. Take a piece of chicken and place it in the mixture. With your fingers, press the chicken into the mixture, turn over, and press again to coat pieces well. In a pan big enough to hold the chicken in a single layer, sauté olive oil and add garlic slices. Add chicken and brown lightly on both sides on medium high heat; (About 3 or 4 minutes per side.)

Pour in beef stock and wine, cover, and bring to a boil. Reduce heat to low and continue cooking, covered, for about 20 minutes. Remove cover, and if necessary, cook a few minutes to reduce sauce; Season to taste with salt and pepper. Remove to a platter and garnish with lemon and parsley if desired.

Update: I received an e-mail from Arlene C., excited that she had found some of Auntie Mimo's treasured recipes. She told me it took a rainy day for her to sift through **fifty years of saved newspaper clippings.**

Original *Chatter Line* newspaper clipping dated September 1979, Carrot Cake Recipe from Auntie Mimo

merican — Sunday, September 2, 1979

Chatter Line

Reader hung

DEAR CHATTERS: I am a crepe lover who is very eager to experiment with crepe recipes of all tyoes. I would be most grateful for any main dish or dessert ideas that call for crepes. Hoping to hear from you. CREPE LOVER

Carrot cake

DEAR CHATTERS: This is one of my favorite recipes; an excellent carrot cake the whole family will enjoy. I have been making it for years and it is always well received.

CARROT CAKE

1	cup granulated sugar
1	egg
1	tsp. vanilla extract
½	cup oil
2	jars (4½oz. size) strained carrot baby food
¼	tsp. baking soda
1	tsp. baking powder
½	tsp. cinnamon
⅛	tsp. nutmeg
1¼	cups all-purpose flour
½	cup chopped nuts
½	cup chopped golden raisins (optional)

Mix sugar, eggs, vanilla, oil and baby food; blend well. Add baking soda, baking powder, cinnamon, nutmeg and flour; mix thoroughly. Fold in nuts and raisins. Pour into a well greased 9 by 5-inch loaf pan. Bake at 350 degrees for 60 to 70 minutes. Test. Cool cake in pan for 10 minutes and then remove to rack to cool completely.

Now comes the hardest part of the entire recipe; do not slice the cake until the next day. It will crumble unless this step is followed.

This is an excellent cake, but be sure to keep it refrigerated. AUNTIE MIMO

Delicious Salad from Talented Home Cook

This recipe was given to me by a woman I worked with who is a tremendous cook and baker. For family and friends she developed a part-time business in her kitchen baking Italian cookies for weddings, showers, etc., huge platters artfully arranged and in demand.

She also has wonderful recipes that she's kept over the years. This recipe for a delicious cold rice salad came from a family affair she attended some fifteen years ago (doesn't know how it was named), and was so well liked she kept it and has served it often; a "tried & true" recipe that keeps being passed along. I have made it several times and someone always asks for the recipe.

Newburyport Rice Salad

INGREDIENTS: *2 packages "Near East Long Grain & Wild Rice"*
1/3 cup raisins
1/3 cup onions (sliced thin)
1 large carrot, shredded
1 red pepper, diced
1 clove garlic, minced
1/3 cup red wine vinegar
2/3 cup vegetable oil (ok to use half vegetable, half olive oil)
1 tablespoon Dijon mustard
½ teaspoon Tabasco sauce

Cook rice per instructions on box, set aside to cool. Mix together raisins, onions, carrots and red pepper, set aside. Mix together garlic, vinegar, oil, mustard and Tabasco sauce. Mix dressing into the rice, than add remaining ingredients. Chill.

Note: 2 cups of cooked chicken or turkey can be added if desired.

CHAPTER 6
TRIED & TRUE

An assortment of recipes that live up to the title of this chapter; recipes that have been used for many years, at times simply given a new twist. You will be entertained and learn new tips and ideas, all intertwined within the chapter as the focus stays on the recipes and at times highlighting one ingredient such as lemons and mangoes.

This chapter "rings" of dependability.

RECIPES:

WISCONSIN LAYERED SALAD
SOPHISTICATED COLE SLAW
SPICED PEACH JAM
COCONUT PECAN SCONES WITH COCONUT GLAZE
PEAR CARAMEL PIE
TUNA NOODLE CASSEROLE TO LOVE
CHOCOLATE-AMARETTO ICE CREAM CAKE
STRAWBERRY TRIFLE
STUFFED CHICKEN BREASTS WITH APRICOT SAUCE
LEMON CHICKEN STIR FRY
MANGO RICE
HOMEMADE HUMMUS

Slow Cooker Recipes:

Mediterranean Roast Turkey
Italian Bread Soup
Yankee Pot Roast with Vegetables
Old Fashioned Applesauce
Apple Streusel Dessert

Raid your Garden or Farmer's Market for this Salad

A wonderful salad that is a meal by itself, full of vegetables, hard cooked eggs and cheddar cheese, plenty of protein in this summer meal. I have been making this for family get-together's since the late 1980's when my sons attended a summer camp in Alton, New Hampshire. . The camp nurse was a friend, as was her husband, the camp athletic director. Their home was in Wisconsin, spending their summers working at the camp. Invited to lunch one hot afternoon, she made this salad, calling it a layered salad. I re-named it Wisconsin Layered Salad, and think of them every time I have it.

Serving suggestion; add crusty rolls, a pitcher of iced tea, and a cool dessert of grilled pineapple slices topped with scoop of coconut ice cream; .best meal ever on a hot summer day.

Wisconsin Layered Salad

INGREDIENTS: *About 4 cups torn lettuce leaves (cover bottom of bowl with a good layer)*
Red onion, 1 small, thinly sliced
1 cucumber, sliced

1 red pepper cut in bite-size strips
2 cups shredded carrots
*1 small bag frozen **baby** peas (do not thaw)*
2 cups mayonnaise
6 hard-cooked eggs
3 to 4 tomatoes, cut in thin quarters
2 cups shredded cheddar cheese
1 large can pitted black olives, sliced
*salt and pepper to taste (I salt and pepper after the eggs and tomato layers.)

In a large salad bowl, layer lettuce on the bottom. (If you have a clear bowl, the layers show through.)

Follow with layers of red onion, cucumber, red pepper, carrots and frozen peas. Spread <u>all</u> the mayonnaise over the peas. Slice eggs and place on top of the mayonnaise. Arrange tomatoes on top of eggs, cover with cheddar cheese. Sprinkle black olives over the top and cover.

Note: You can replace mayonnaise with half sour cream, half Greek yogurt, half lite mayonnaise, or with a thick creamy salad dressing such as Marie's brand.

Comment from Marilyn, Bradford Massachusetts: *I have made your layered salad a few times now for family barbecues and it is well liked; my daughters insist on it.*

Comment from "G" in Pelham New Hampshire: *I made the Wisconsin layered salad for one of our Senior events and everyone asked for the recipe; it was very refreshing on a hot day and filling.*

This is a deliciously different take on Cole slaw that won a Blue Ribbon years ago in a recipe contest highlighting cabbage. I find this recipe a must to serve with ribs and fish tacos.

Sophisticated Cole Slaw

INGREDIENTS: *4 cups shredded green cabbage*

1 cup shredded red cabbage

¼ cup chopped onion (red or Vidalia)

*2 jalapeno chili peppers, seeded and **finely** chopped*

2 tablespoons chopped fresh cilantro

8 ounces whole kernel corn (fresh, cut off cooked cob is best)

*¼ cup **each** of chopped red and green bell pepper*

4 ounces (1 cup) shredded white cheese (cheddar or montery jack)

SALAD DRESSING; *¾ cup mayonnaise*

1/2 cup sour cream

2 tablespoons fresh lime juice

1 teaspoon cumin

½ teaspoon sugar

¼ teaspoon each; salt, pepper

Combine all salad ingredients in a large bowl.

Combine all dressing ingredients, blending well. Pour over salad, toss to coat. 6-8 servings

Comments from Susan N. *Last week my family and I enjoyed your sophisticated cole slaw so much that it will become a regular addition. I struggle to make good food with fresh veggies that the kids and my husband will like. You have given us some good recipes and I need to start my own recipe book with about ten of them. I also like to read your personal anecdotes that are touching and interesting.*

FAMILY RECIPE FOR JAM NOW IN SON AND DAUGHTER-IN-LAW'S HANDS

For several years I have received a jar of this peach jam from my cousin Paul. He and his wife Carol have one "dwarf" peach tree that Paul says generally provides enough fruit to make about eight batches of jam. When asked if there is any history to the recipe, he says it originally was his mother's, who says she "concocted" it herself, believing the spices would be a good match for the peaches, and Paul strongly agrees.

Paul and Carol's batch (both enjoy making it), is so loved by their daughter and her family, husband and three young granddaughters, that they use 32 ounce preserve jars, as well as pretty 4 ounce. jars for gifts. I lucked out, coming home with a 32 oz. jar!

It doesn't last long though with one of my sisters who loves it stirred into plain yogurt.

SPICED PEACH JAM

INGREDIENTS: *4 cups fully ripe peaches (peel, pit, mash/crush)*
¼ cup lemon juice
7 and ½ cups sugar
½ teaspoon EACH; cinnamon, cloves, and allspice
2nd step....1 pouch of Certo liquid pectin

Combine all <u>except</u> Certo in large pan. Mix well and bring to a full rolling boil. Boil hard for 1 minute stirring constantly. Remove from heat and stir in 1 pouch of Certo immediately. Stir for 5 more minutes (skim if needed). Put in jam jars and proceed with 10 minute boiling water "bath" to seal canning jars. Let cool and make sure the jars are properly sealed.

Paul and Carol state they use a food processor, feeling it makes a better jam as well as being easier. If you have one, put the peeled, pitted peaches in the processor with the lemon juice and "pulse" until fully chopped and incorporated.

Coconut Scones a Winner, Literally

I'm always looking for good recipes. But this time I wasn't looking. A friend saw this in a national magazine several years ago and right away thought of me. Most everyone knows I love coconut; one of my "faves" in life.

I have had coconut many different ways; cakes, coffee-cake, cookies, but never scones. My taste buds were piqued especially since pecans were included in the recipe. I had only made scones once before, but that did not intimidate me. There was no way I wasn't going to have these scones. For a person that collects cookbooks and recipes, the piece de resistance was that this recipe was the winner in a coconut themed contest the magazine ran.

For me personally, I am always looking for ways to lighten up recipes; less sugar, and lower fat. When I made these, there is not a lot of sugar to begin with so I left that as is and tried to lower the cholesterol and fat. I experimented by substituting two egg whites for two of the eggs. I also substituted fat-free Greek yogurt(less watery), and sugar-free applesauce for **half** of the butter. I omitted the sprinkling of sugar on the tops, and put as little confectioners' sugar as possible in the glaze. This worked for me, and as I have said before, cooking is often personalized per our needs; sometimes less salt, often less fat, sugar, and calories.

When I make these scones for company I go for the gold and use this original recipe, and I am in heaven.

Coconut-Pecan Scones with Coconut Glaze

Preheat oven to 400 degrees.

INGREDIENTS: *4 ¼ cups all purpose flour*
2 tablespoons baking powder
1 teaspoon salt
¼ cup sugar, plus more for sprinkling
2 cups fresh shredded coconut
3 sticks cold unsalted butter, cubed
1 cup unsweetened coconut milk
4 large eggs, lightly beaten
1 teaspoon coconut extract
1 and ½ to 2 cups finely chopped pecans, per your liking
GLAZE: *2 tablespoons unsweetened coconut milk*
¼ teaspoon coconut extract
¼ teaspoon vanilla extract
½ to 1 cup confectioners' sugar

Line 2 baking sheets with parchment paper. Whisk flour, baking powder, salt, granulated sugar, and coconut in a bowl. Beat in butter with mixer on low speed, then raise speed to high and beat until mixture coarse crumbs.

In another bowl, whisk coconut milk, eggs, and coconut extract together, stir into the flour mixture just until combined. Stir in pecans; careful to not over mix.

Scoop 2-3 inch mounds of dough onto prepared baking sheets (I use a large ice cream scoop). Sprinkle tops with a very small amount of sugar and bake until light golden brown, 14to17 minutes.

Make glaze by whisking coconut milk, both extracts, and ½ cup confectioners' sugar until smooth, adding more sugar to thicken. Drizzle over scones while still slightly warm. (Makes 16to20)

Fall Baking; Start with Pear Caramel Pie

Pears have become as versatile as the apple in our kitchens; adding a special touch to salads, soups, and main dishes, as well as desserts galore. Make pear chutney to top pork chops, substitute pears in a favorite apple cake, or toss in a salad with greens, walnuts, dried cranberries and cheese of your choice.

A special lunch salad is easy: place a peeled, cored, softened pear -half on a small bed of greens. Roll an ounce of goat cheese into a ball and roll in chopped nuts; place in center of pear half. Sprinkle with balsamic vinegar and honey.

At this time of the year I think back to my grandparents who had a Bartlett pear tree in their back yard. My grandfather babied that tree and it produced a lot of pears; I can remember him picking a bushel of them, and my grandmother making her special pear pie.

Each Sunday night when we had supper at their house, Nana would invariably make the usual tomato soup and grilled cheese sandwiches, switching dessert from apple pie to pear pie in the Fall months. As children, I remember the occasional grumbling we did, "tomato soup again.", but years later those Sunday evenings with grilled cheese and tomato soup, and her pies, invoke warm memories that I will always treasure.

PEAR CARAMEL PIE

Preheat oven 375 degrees 9" pie plate

Use your favorite pie crust recipe for a double crust pie, (see Chapter 1> pastry)

or purchase pre-made pie crusts such as Pillsbury brand.

FILLING:
8 cups pears, peeled and thinly sliced
½ cup packed light brown sugar
½ teaspoon nutmeg
½ cup sugar
½ teaspoon salt
2 tablespoons flour
1 tablespoon lemon juice
1 teaspoon cinnamon
½ teaspoon vanilla
4 tablespoons heavy cream
3 tablespoons unsalted butter

Sprinkle pears with lemon juice.
Combine dry ingredients in large bowl and add pears. Toss to mix. Add vanilla and cream. Melt butter in heavy fry pan. Add fruit mixture and cook 7 to 9 minutes to **slightly** soften pears.
Spoon mixture into pie plate lined with bottom crust.
Place top crust on, pinch crusts together. Cut a few slits in top crust to vent. Bake 45 to 60 minutes till pears feel soft when pierced with a fork.

Note: May substitute apples to make Apple Caramel Pie

A Tuna Noodle Casserole to Love? Believe it.

Gourmet, maybe not; comfortable, delicious, and classic, absolutely!

Casseroles, baked in a casserole dish such as the old favorite, glass Pyrex, are hot and creamy and usually have cheese. They can be main courses or sides, and are always welcome at a potluck gathering. To me, it is a way to share a piece of yourself, as a casserole makes any dinner table a bit more colorful and interesting. Casseroles are favorites because there are so many concoctions and variations to any one recipe that you can have a little culinary fun. Many casserole recipes can be prepared the night before or the morning of, kept refrigerated, and put in the oven to bake when you get home in the evening.

This recipe comes from a friend of forty years. April developed it herself, very often not using a recipe for a lot of her cooking. It took us a while to sit down and put it in recipe form. April is amazing to me, as I am a cook who needs a recipe to follow. (Her scalloped potatoes are another of her "throw it together" fantastic dishes). Besides being a very good cook and baker (desserts her specialty), she has celebrated thirty-eight years as a valued nurse and employee at the Milford Regional Medical Center in Milford, Massachusetts.

I suggest that the first time you make this, use this basic recipe so you can truly appreciate the flavors (no fishy taste here). Next time feel free to put in your favorite ad-ins like peas, onions, ham, etc.., personalizing it to your family's tastes.

Tuna Noodle Casserole
Recipe courtesy of April Hawkins, Milford Massachusetts

Prepare a 13x9x2" baking pan; butter or coat with cooking spray

Preheat oven to 350 degrees

INGREDIENTS: *Egg noodles, x -wide - 18 ounces (Use 1 full 12 ounce bag and half of another)*
1 (12 ounce) can tuna fish (Bumble Bee packed in water good), drained and crumbled
1 (8 ounce) block Velveeta cheese, cubed
1 stick (1/2 cup) butter
1/3 cup all-purpose flour
2 cups whole milk (may use 1%, half & half, or partial amount light cream); this depends on how rich you would like the sauce to be.
1 teaspoon black pepper

Cook noodles according to package directions in salted water. Drain well in colander.

Make béchamel sauce (also known as white sauce):
In same pan you used to cook noodles melt 1 stick of butter over medium heat; add flour, stirring constantly with a wooden spoon. Slowly add milk stirring constantly. Add pepper. Continue to stir while adding cubed cheese; sauce will thicken as it cooks.
Add crumbled tuna, stirring well.
Mix in cooked noodles. (Add salt to taste here, only if desired)

If mixture too thick, stir in up to a cup of milk to thin.
Pour mixture into prepared pan.

TOPPING: *Panko bread crumbs (approximately 1 cup)*
1 stick butter

Cover top of casserole with panko crumbs, drizzle with butter.

Bake for 45 minutes until hot and bubbly.

Comments from Bonita C.: *Kudos to April. I wanted something filling and meatless for supper and this solved my dilemma. I followed your advice and didn't add anything and it's true I could appreciate the flavors. It brought me back to the 1950's and 60's and the comfort of a good old-fashioned casserole. This recipe is a keeper. My sister lives in Shreveport LA and tells me Velveeta is a staple in most Southern kitchens.*

Ice Cream Cake Brings ooh's and aahs

Here's a little trivia you might enjoy. Where is the ice cream capital of the WORLD?

Believe it or not in a small city (population 10,000), Lemars, Iowa; In 1994 it was officially recognized as the ice cream capital of the world as it produces the most ice cream.

Known as Blue Bunny brand, it had its modest beginnings as a dairy farm with only 15 cows in 1913.

Turning to this delicious concoction, which is a surprisingly easy ice cream cake to make with a distinct homemade flavor. If you don't have a 9" springform pan, this summer dessert is worth having one.

This recipe comes from an interesting cookbook published in 1993. Hundreds of community cookbooks were collected nationwide from all kinds of organizations; churches, hospital auxiliaries, clubs, etc. (I love those little cookbooks, good home cooking). Thousands of recipes were tested and rated till the cream of the crop was chosen for the book.

This particular recipe comes from a Medical Ctr. Auxiliary in Fort Oglethorpe, GA. that published their cook book-let for fundraising.

CHOCOLATE AMARETTO ICE CREAM CAKE

INGREDIENTS: *1 and ½ cups chocolate wafer or cookie crumbs*
½ cup slivered almonds, toasted and crushed
1/3 cup butter or margarine, melted
4 (1 ounce) squares semisweet chocolate, melted
¼ cup amaretto
1 (14 ounce) can sweetened condensed milk
1 (8 ounce) carton sour cream
3 cups whipping cream, whipped
Optional - additional whipped cream for garnish

Combine chocolate wafer crumbs, almonds, and butter; firmly press 1 cup of crumb mixture in bottom of a lightly greased 9-inch spring form pan. If you don't have a spring form pan, use a 9inch deep dish pie or cake pan, which has been lined with waxed paper, so it can be lifted out onto a serving plate.
Set prepared crust and remaining crumb mixture aside.

Combine chocolate and amaretto in a large bowl; stir well. Add sweetened condensed milk and sour cream; stir well. Fold in whipped cream. Spoon half of chocolate mixture into prepared crust; sprinkle with half of reserved crumb mixture. Repeat procedure with remaining chocolate mixture and crumbs. Cover and freeze at least 8 hours. Carefully remove sides of spring form pan. Let stand 10 minutes before serving. Garnish each serving with a dollop of whipped cream if desired. This makes approx. 8-10 servings.

STUFFED CHICKEN BREASTS WITH APRICOT SAUCE

A co-worker shared this recipe with me more than twelve years ago. I have made it many times, especially Sunday dinners and when I have company. It is one of those meals that is perfect when you want something a little special but still informal. When I serve this for company, I follow the recipe as is. If for a weekday supper, I omit the apricots and almonds.

I sometimes use only three-quarters of the sixteen- ounce bottle of dressing, and three-quarters of a small jar apricot preserves, so that it makes less sauce. I also have used low fat, low calorie russian dressing and low-sugar apricot preserves, and we have liked that also.

You will have to try it first and then make any changes to your liking. But I can say with confidence this is a keeper recipe. I serve this with rice as this makes a lot of a sauce, and I love it served with homemade rice pilaf.

INGREDIENTS: *4 whole chicken breasts, boneless and skinless*
1 small box prepared stuffing mix, prepared according to box directions
1/4 cup finely chopped dates
1/2 cup each... chopped dried apricots and almond slices

While making stuffing, simmer together in small pan:
1 (16 ounce) bottle Ken's Russian dressing (any brand will do)
1 small jar apricot preserves
1 packet dry onion soup mix

Pound the chicken till about ½ inch thin. Add dried fruit and almonds to the prepared stuffing. Stuff chicken by putting a good-size scoop of stuffing on a lightly greased baking pan (use a deep baking pan), place a chicken breast on top, tucking it under the stuffing. Salt and pepper as you like. Pour sauce over all and bake at 350 degrees for about 45to50 minutes. Baste with sauce a few times during cooking.

If you want to serve a special dessert for a company dinner, this is it. I liked it with orange liqueur.

CREAMY TRIFLE

INGREDIENTS: *One (10 ounce) angel loaf cake*
½ cup strawberry jam
1/3 cup orange juice, liqueur, or cream sherry
3 cups strawberries, hulled and cut in thirds or halved
1 cup whipping cream
2 tablespoons white powdered sugar
1 teaspoon vanilla extract
2 tablespoons sliced almonds, toasted; optional

Custard Sauce: Mix 1 ½ tablespoons cornstarch with ½ cup milk. In a heavy saucepan or double boiler, heat 1¾ cups milk with ¼ cup sugar just to boiling. Remove from heat. Stir in cornstarch mixture until smooth; cook, stirring constantly until thickened. Simmer 3 minutes. Remove from heat. Beat in 1 teaspoon vanilla extract then 3 beaten egg yolks. Cover. Chill.

TO PREPARE:

1. Make custard sauce and refrigerate.

2. Split cake into 3 layers. Spread jam between layers and reassemble layers. Cut into 2 inch cubes. Arrange cubes in a 2 quart trifle bowl or serving bowl. Sprinkle with orange juice or orange liqueur or cream sherry.

3. Spoon sliced strawberries over cake.

4. Pour chilled custard sauce or pudding over berries. Cover and refrigerate for 1 hour.

5. Whip cream till thickened, add sugar and vanilla. Whip till stiff peaks.

6. Pipe or spread whipped cream over custard. Garnish with whole strawberries.

Sprinkle with toasted almonds if desired. Chill.

Note: I added blueberries when I made this for a Memorial Day get-together.

Lemon Goodness

Dotted with lots of zesty lemon, this tasty stir-fry has a colorful mix of snow peas, carrots, and scallions. Feel free to substitute other thinly sliced vegetables, such as green peppers or zucchini. I like to serve this over rice noodles or brown rice.

Lemon Chicken Stir-Fry

INGREDIENTS: *1 lemon*
½ cup reduced sodium chicken broth
3 tablespoons reduced sodium soy sauce

2 teaspoons cornstarch

1 tablespoon olive oil

1 pound boneless, skinless chicken breasts cut into 1 inch pieces

10 ounces mushrooms, halved or quartered

1 cup sliced carrots, cut on the diagonal

2 cups snow peas, stems and strings removed if fresh

1 bunch scallions, cut into 1 inch pieces; white and green parts separated

1 tablespoon chopped garlic

Grate 1 teaspoon lemon zest and set aside. Juice the lemon and whisk 3 tablespoons of the juice with broth, soy sauce and cornstarch in a small bowl.

Heat oil in a large skillet over medium-high heat; add chicken and cook, stirring occasionally, until just cooked through, 4 to 5 minutes. Transfer to a plate. Add mushrooms and carrots to the pan and cook until carrots are just tender, about 5 minutes. Add snow peas, scallion whites, garlic and the reserved lemon zest; Cook and stir until fragrant, 30 seconds. Whisk broth mixture and add to pan; cook, stirring until thickened, 2 to 3 minutes. Add scallion greens, chicken and any accumulated juices; cook, stirring, until well heated, another few minutes. Serves 4

WAYS WITH LEMON:

1. Basic glaze; whisk 2 cups confectioners' sugar with 2 tablespoons fresh lemon juice; add up to 2 more tablespoons juice until desired consistency; good on pound cake, cookies, coffee cake.

2. Lemony smashed potatoes ; Lightly smash 3 pounds cooked red un-peeled potatoes, toss with a quarter cup olive oil and 2 teaspoons grated lemon zest; add coarse salt and pepper to taste.

3. Lemon-chive roasted vegetables; Cut potatoes, carrots, parsnips, and sweet onions in large pieces. Place in bowl and coat with chopped fresh chives, lemon zest and juice, salt, pepper, and just enough olive oil to coat all. (Start with a teaspoon of zest and a couple tablespoons lemon juice to taste.) Bake at 425 degrees in a single layer for approximately 30 minutes.

4. Fresh green beans with lemon and thyme: To 2 pounds cooked green beans add 2 tablespoons melted butter, two teaspoons chopped fresh thyme, and 1 teaspoon finely grated lemon peel. Mix well.

5. Lemon water: Keep a large pitcher of ice water with sliced lemons in it in your refrigerator all summer to promote hydrating with water and healthy lemons.

JUICE & ZEST

1. Juicing a lemon; to get the most juice from a lemon, start by rolling it on a work surface under your palm a few times, or microwave it for 10 seconds before cutting it in half. Thin-skinned lemons have more juice and fewer seeds. Look for round lemons that give slightly when pressed.

2. Get the best zest; a microplane grater is the easiest way to get fine zest, and it is easier to clean than a box grater. For larger pieces of zest for cocktails or candy, use a vegetable peeler. Thick-skinned lemons are obviously better for zesting. Scrub lemons before using to remove food-grade wax from skin. When zesting try to only get the yellow part not the white "pith" which is bitter.

ALL ABOUT MANGOES

Mangoes are cause for celebration in Florida. I was amazed to learn of several Mango *festivals* in June and July every year that are enjoyed by thousands.

A huge event is at the Fairchild Tropical Botanic Garden in Coral Gables which holds their mango festival every summer. This popular three day event includes chefs preparing gourmet meals, mango tastings, and even mango vendors selling everything mango related from mango ice cream, cakes, even wine.

Free samples of Mango salsa, mango cake, and mango creampuffs are offered. Local bakers and chefs sign cook-books and talk to patrons. Local soap makers bring mango soap, along with many other kinds to choose from.

A catering service hands out mango cannolis while promoting their service. A pie maker from Georgia offers samples of delicious mango pie.

Because this is a Botanical Garden, I was fascinated to know that a multitude of mango trees are for sale; people line up to buy different varieties of mango trees every year at this event.

MANGO RICE

INGREDIENTS: *2 tablespoons butter or margarine, melted*
2 tablespoons chopped onion
½ cup white long-grain rice, uncooked
1 cup chicken broth
1 ¼ cup diced fresh mango
1/8 th teaspoon fresh ground nutmeg
1/8 th teaspoon fresh ground black pepper
¼ cup slivered almonds, toasted

Add salt to taste

Sauté onion in butter in a medium saucepan over medium heat; add rice, stirring well, stir in broth. Bring to a boil; cover, reduce heat, simmer about 20 minutes or until liquid is absorbed. Stir in remaining ingredients. Let sit for 10 minutes and serve; makes four servings.

About mangoes:

1.   Mangoes from Mexico: Basically kidney shaped, greenish yellow, in supermarkets March to September.

2.   Mangoes from Florida: Available May through September. Most popular variety is the *"Tommy Atkins"* which is colorful with an orange/red skin; Sweet and juicy, a bit more fibrous than other varieties.

Hayden mango usually runs less than a pound, is rounder than most varieties, and has a green to yellow skin with a red blush. The flesh is firm and bright orange with a good rich flavor. *Keith* mango is round and very fat, the largest of the Florida mangoes, usually 2 to 3 pounds. It has mostly green skin. People think it is not ripe when it actually is. The pit is smaller. The Keith mango has a full flavor which is tart and lemony, and smooth fiber-free flesh. The *Kent* mango is large, fat, and not as oval; it has a green skin with a reddish cheek. Its yellow- gold flesh is very juicy and fiber-free.

Palmer mango is long, oval-shaped and has rosy, speckled skin with orange-yellow flesh. It's very sweet and is fibrous only around the pit. The Palmer has a little less of the tropical taste of most

Mangoes, with a flavor more like that of a nectarine or peach.

Mangoes from Haiti - Usually flat and elongated, with a skin that starts out lime green and ripens to yellow. It doesn't look pretty, and the flesh is a little more fibrous, but it has great flavor, an intense, tropical taste. It's a great winter treat in January, when the season begins, and it ripens very well at home.

Season lasts till September.

3. If you have an under-ripe mango and you want to use it right away, put it on the grill or into a fry pan for a few minutes; the heat caramelizes the natural sugars of the fruit and brings out the juiciness.

4. To deal with that big pit, trim one end flat, stand fruit upright, slice around the pit on either side.

5. Also, mango splitters, which are similar to apple corers, cost about $10 and work great.

(I bought mine at Target a few years ago and wouldn't be without it).

Keep in mind that one of the best ways to use mangoes is in salads.

Two delicious salads to make:

1) Add sliced mangoes to a salad of greens, chicken strips, broccoli florets, and crumbled blue cheese,

2) Add mangoes to a salad of spinach greens, sliced avocado, andsalted peanuts, with an olive oil/lime juice dressing.

"WRAP IT UP" WITH HOMEMADE HUMMUS

I was introduced to hummus by a friend of many years. April is of Lebanese descent where hummus is a staple in their diet. Growing up in the 1960's she watched her Aunts cook traditional Lebanese foods and learned from each of them. April makes terrific lamb kibbeh and stuffed grape leaves, for years growing a huge grape vine in her backyard, insuring fresh grape leaves when she needed them.

It was early in our friendship when I first had April's homemade hummus which she serves with a basket of Syrian bread, torn into large pieces (red onion and olive oil on the side). Hummus is easy to make in the blender and keeps well in the refrigerator.

Hummus has been primarily served as an appetizer/snack; now it is being used often as a substitute for mayonnaise in sandwiches, as in the wrap recipes here.

HUMMUS

INGREDIENTS: *2 (16 ounce) cans chickpeas (also called garbanzo beans),*
drained and rinsed
½ cup water
Juice of one lemon
5 tablespoons tahini (sesame paste)
3 cloves garlic, crushed
¼ cup olive oil
Wraps:
8 (8 inch) whole wheat tortillas
3 carrots, peeled and shredded (about 2 cups)
Greens of choice
1 cup shredded part-skim mozzarella

Make hummus:

In a blender or food processor, puree chickpeas, water, lemon juice, garlic, and tahini. With machine running, add olive oil slowly while pureeing until silky smooth, about 45 to 50 seconds.

Keep refrigerated in an airtight container.

Carrots, Greens, and Hummus Wraps

On each tortilla, spread 2 tablespoons hummus slightly below the center, keeping the sides clear. Top hummus with ¼ cup shredded carrots, ½ cup torn greens, and 2 tablespoons shredded cheese; roll bottom of tortilla over the ingredients. Fold sides in and finish rolling up tortilla. Slice diagonally. If packing for lunch, wrap in foil or waxed paper.

GRILLED CHICKEN WRAP WITH HUMMUS

FOR 1 WRAP: *½ of a grilled, boneless chicken breast (seasoned per your preference)*
Favorite wrap
3 tablespoons hummus
Lettuce leaves, tomato slices, sliced red onion, sliced black olives (all or your choice)

Cut chicken into thin slices. Spread hummus on wrap. Place lettuce, tomato slices and sliced chicken on top of hummus. Roll the wrap and enjoy!

Comments from *Suzanne and family: I never made hummus before, but decided to try it after seeing your recipe.*

My husband, son and daughter love hummus and I am always buying it. Your recipe was easy and now I have made it again and doubled the recipe this time. My husband and son like it with chips and my daughter likes it with celery sticks.

Slow Cooker a Kitchen Necessity

Several of my best recipes are Crockpot recipes. Your slow cooker recipes are probably standby's that have become family favorites. In this section I hope you find a new favorite slow cooker recipe to enjoy making and serving.

Crock pots were introduced in the 1970's, named that due to the insert being crockery. They were re-made in the mid 1990's with a new name, slow cooker, as many inserts then and now are stainless steel. Regarding slow cooker capacity, the average size is in the five quart range. A large slow-cooker is six and a half to seven quart capacity. They come in round or oval shape. I prefer the oval model, but it is a personal preference.

Considering the hectic pace of today's lifestyle, it is no wonder many people use this kitchen helper. Not only can you have a hot meal ready when you get home in the evening, it uses less electricity than the oven, less fat than frying, and my favorite, it doesn't heat up the kitchen in the summer.

Tips for cooking in a slow cooker:

1. Save expensive meat cuts for grilling or broiling. In-expensive cuts come out fork-tender in a crock pot.

Trim fat where you can.

2. Remove skin from chicken unless you have browned it first. (Chicken wings exempt)

3. Add dairy products near end of cooking time (last 40 minutes) so they do not curdle.

4. Start with room temperature foods if at all possible.

5. Most recipes are for 4to5 quart cookers. Using a 6 or 7 quart cooker will be fine.

6. Have vegetables prepped the night before for quicker preparation in the morning.

MEDITERRANEAN ROAST TURKEY

INGREDIENTS: *2 cups chopped onion (1 large)*
½ cup pitted kalamata olives
½ cup julienne-cut drained, oil-packed sun-dried to-mato halves
2 tablespoons fresh lemon juice
1 ½ teaspoons bottled minced garlic
1 teaspoon Greek seasoning mix (recipe below)
½ teaspoon **of each**; *salt and freshly ground black pepper*
1 (4 pound) boneless turkey breast
½ cup chicken broth, divided
3 tablespoons all-purpose flour

In slow cooker, combine all ingredients except broth and flour.

Add ¼ cup of the chicken broth. Cover and cook on low for 7 hours.

Then, combine remaining quarter cup of chicken broth and flour in a small bowl, stir with a whisk until smooth. Add broth mixture to slow cooker. Cover and cook on LOW for 30 minutes. Cut turkey into slices; Makes 6to8 servings with approximate half- cup servings of onion/broth mixture on side, which is good served over mashed potatoes.

GREEK SEASONING MIX: *2 teaspoons dried oregano*
2 teaspoons salt

1 ½ teaspoons onion powder
1 ½ teaspoons garlic powder
1 teaspoon cornstarch
1 teaspoon black pepper
1 teaspoon dried parsley flakes
1 teaspoon paprika
½ teaspoon ground cinnamon½ teaspoon
    ground nutmeg
½ teaspoon thyme

Keep in airtight container; Makes ¼ cup.

Good on poultry, lamb, roasted vegetables.

This is a hearty soup that is colorful and fresh tasting. In Italy this is known as "Ribollita" and is almost a staple in many Italian homes.

I love making soups in a slow cooker due to the low heat and long period of cooking time. The ingredients blend together and every bit of flavor comes out while the house smells delightful.

You will find yourself making this soup often; no browning, just throw everything in the pot.

ITALIAN BREAD SOUP

INGREDIENTS: *½ large onion*
          1 large carrot
          2 ribs celery
          2 cloves garlic
          ½ pound dried navy beans (1 and ¼ cups)
          2 quarts vegetable stock or water

1 bay leaf

1 sprig dried or fresh rosemary

1 large head escarole (may substitute spinach or kale)
stemmed and chopped coarsely

2 thick slices (day old) crusty Italian bread (ciabatta or
panella good), cut into 1 inch cubes (about 4 cups)

2 ripe tomatoes, chopped

½ bunch flat-leaf parsley, stemmed and chopped

salt and pepper to taste

3 tablespoons extra virgin olive oil

Coarsely chop onion, carrot, celery, and garlic and place in slow cooker. Add beans, stock, bay leaf, and rosemary; cook, covered, on low setting for 5 hours, until beans are tender. Add escarole, bread cubes, tomatoes, and parsley, and stir gently to mix greens into liquid. Cover the cooker, put on high setting, and cook for another 30 to 40 minutes, or until greens tender and soup hot.

I add plenty of black pepper at this point, (personal choice). Remove bay leaf and rosemary stem if used.

Makes 4to 5 servings Serve in deep bowls; drizzle with oil.

YANKEE POT ROAST withVEGETABLES

INGREDIENTS: *2 and ½ to 3 pound chuck pot roast*

3 medium/large potatoes scrubbed and left unpeeled.
Cut into halves or thirds

4-5 large carrots cut into 1 inch pieces

3-4 parsnips cut into 1 inch pieces

1 large onion, cut into wedges

2 bay leaves
1 teaspoon dried rosemary
3/4 teaspoon dried thyme
3/4 cup beef broth

Trim excess fat from meat. Cut meat into large serving pieces; sprinkle with salt and pepper. Place vegetables, bay leaves, and seasonings into slow cooker, toss to mix. Place beef on top, pour broth over. (The beef will make more juice as it cooks) Cover and cook on low 8 1/2 to 9 hours. Remove and discard bay leaves. Makes 5 to 6 servings.

Note: If you want to serve bread with this, brown bread is a traditional "Yankee" accompaniment.

Old-Fashioned Applesauce

Use at least a 4-quart crock-pot (slow cooker)

INGREDIENTS: *3 pounds red apples (8 or 9 medium); washed, cored,*
        peeled & sliced
        ¼ cup packed brown sugar
        juice and grated zest of 1 lemon
        1 teaspoon ground cinnamon (or 2 cinnamon sticks)
        ½ teaspoon nutmeg
        ¼ teaspoon ground cloves

Place apples in crock-pot. Combine remaining ingredients in a bowl with ½ cup water and stir to dissolve sugar. Pour over apples, stirring to coat them. Cover and cook on **low** setting for 4 hours, pushing the apples down into the liquid a couple of times during the last hour of cooking.

You can leave the applesauce "chunky", or you can press through a strainer to make it smooth. (Peels can be left on if you strain it or put through a food mill; it will retain a pinkish color). Makes close to 3 pints

APPLE STREUSEL DESSERT

INGREDIENTS: *6 cups peeled, sliced apples*
1 ¼ teaspoons cinnamon
*¼ teaspoon **each**; allspice and nutmeg*
¾ cup milk
2 tablespoons soft butter
¾ cup sugar
2 eggs
1 teaspoon vanilla extract
½ cup biscuit/baking mix (such as Bisquick brand)

In large bowl, toss apples with cinnamon, allspice, and nutmeg. Place in greased slow cooker.

In mixing bowl, combine milk, butter, sugar, eggs, vanilla and baking mix; blend well, spoon over apples.

TOPPING: *1 cup biscuit/baking mix*
1/3 cup packed brown sugar
3 tablespoons cold butter
½ cup sliced almonds, optional

For topping combine biscuit mix and brown sugar in a bowl; cut in cold butter until crumbly. Stir in almonds. Sprinkle mixture over apples. Cover and cook on low for 6 to7 hours until apples are tender.

Serve warm with whipped cream or vanilla ice cream

CHAPTER 7
JUST SALADS

<u>Dinner Salads</u>

CHICKEN CAESAR
WHITE BEAN, TUNA AND AVOCADO
CURRY SALMON SALAD
FAMOUS AUTHENTIC COBB SALAD
TROPICAL CHICKEN SALAD
<u>LUNCH AND SIDE SALADS</u> CRANBERRY SPINACH SALAD
WARM LEEK, ASPARAGUS & POTATO SALAD
SUGAR SNAP PEA & CHERRY TOMATO PASTA SALAD
ASPARAGUS PASTA SALAD WITH ORANGE AND MINT
<u>SALADS HIGHLIGHTING FRUIT</u>: APPLE WALNUT SALAD
AVOCADO SALAD WITH HONEYDEW & FONTINA
SALAD GREENS WITH STRAWBERRIES & GOAT CHEESE
DELICIOUS CITRUS SALAD
<u>HOMEMADE DRESSINGS</u>: RANCH
VINAIGRETTE WITH CUMIN & MINT
BASIC LEMON VINAIGRETTE
BALSAMIC ROSEMARY VINAIGRETTE

GONE ARE THE DAYS OF A BORING SALAD

Today's salads are colorful and loaded with healthy ingredients. We all know we should be eating healthy, and speaking for myself, I can eat salad daily but only when I can vary the ingredients.

Even with salad, portions are important. I enjoy salads, but I have to be careful not to overdo ingredients such as cheeses, nuts, dried fruits, croutons, and dressings that are high fat with sugar added.

In this chapter I have provided recipes for lighter dressings and how to make your own healthier croutons.

If you love cheese on your salad, but want to keep it to a healthy amount, try Fontina cheese.

Remember, **don't go without**; just think and do differently.

Enjoy Dinner Salads Year-Round:

Most common of dinner salads is the Chicken Caesar which is an all-time favorite of mine and my family.

In this first section I will introduce a few alternative dinner salads as well as homemade salad dressings.

"Dinner Salads" can be very substantial and healthy as well.

And in the heat of summer I do not want a heavy meal and enjoy these salads that require minimum cooking as an added benefit.

This Caesar salad is different from the traditional as no oil is used in the dressing, only a small amount of light mayonnaise. Tangy low-fat buttermilk provides a zippy flavor as it tenderizes the chicken.

Making your own croutons saves on calories and adds a fresh home-made taste.

Chicken Caesar Salad

Serves 4

INGREDIENTS: *3 boneless, skinless chicken breast halves, lightly seasoned with salt and pepper*
Marinade/dressing:
1 ½ cups low-fat buttermilk
2 tablespoons fresh lemon juice
1 garlic clove, finely minced
¼ cup parmesan cheese

In medium bowl, combine buttermilk, lemon juice, garlic, and parmesan.

Place chicken in a resealable plastic bag.

Reserve ½ cup buttermilk mixture for dressing salad.

Add chicken to remaining mixture.

Refrigerate chicken a minimum of 15 minutes and up to 10 hours.

Line baking sheet with aluminum foil. Transfer chicken to baking sheet, discard marinade. Broil 4 inches from heat, about 14-16 minutes. Let rest 5 minutes, and thinly slice. Cover and set aside.

Croutons: Purchase store-bought or make your own with 2 slices of multigrain or whole wheat bread. Brush each side of bread lightly with olive oil and season with salt and pepper. Place on baking sheet lined with aluminum foil and broil until toasted, 1 to 2 minutes per side; cut into 1 inch pieces.

Assemble Salad:

In a large bowl, place reserved buttermilk mixture. Add ¼ cup light mayonnaise and stir to mix.

Add 2 medium heads of romaine lettuce, cut into pieces, and half of a small head radicchio, thinly sliced.

Add chicken and croutons; toss to combine. Serve immediately.

Reader's reviews

I tried your recipe for Chicken Caesar Salad, and it was really good. The salad dressing was so different made with buttermilk, light mayo and parmesan cheese. A lot less calories I think and a zippy flavor. **Tom, Atkinson NH**

A while back you sent me your recipe for Chicken Caesar Salad. Just letting you know it was delicious and will be a regular at our dinner table. Going to try your Ranch dressing with Green Salad next. Your thoughtfulness in sending these is much appreciated. **David**

This dinner salad is diabetic friendly and all-around healthy.

WHITE BEAN, TUNA, AND AVOCADO SALAD

Serves 4

INGREDIENTS: *1 can (12 ounce) solid white albacore tuna, drained well*
½ cup diced red onion
1 tablespoon **each** *of the following: chopped fresh basil, chopped fresh chives,*
Extra virgin olive oil, fresh lemon juice, red wine vinegar
1/2 teaspoon kosher salt
1/2 teaspoon black pepper
1 cup cannelloni beans, rinsed and drained

1/2 cup diced tomato
4 cups salad greens
2 medium avocados

In a medium bowl, flake tuna with a fork. Stir in onion, basil, chives, oil, lemon juice, vinegar, salt and pepper. Fold in beans and tomato.

Divide greens over 4 individual salad plates. Cut avocados in half, remove pits and remove some of the avocado flesh from skin using a large spoon.

Place 1 avocado half over greens on each plate. Fold removed avocado into tuna mixture and spoon into avocado shells, spilling over onto greens.

Optional: For a Tuscan addition to this salad toast a thinly sliced French baguette, brush with olive oil, and serve with salad.

The first time I had this salad was on a trip to Connecticut to visit an Aunt and Uncle who are well aware of my love for salmon but were not aware that curry is one of my favorite spices.

My Aunt Jane and Uncle Bob had spent thirty-four years in Alaska, and I was lucky enough to visit them and become acquainted with this beautiful state and freshly caught "copper river reds", salmon.

Once you have had fresh caught salmon; it is hard to settle for anything else, but I have learned to like canned salmon, especially if it is processed and canned in Alaska. Alaska canned salmon is great in salads, casseroles, and salmon chowder. Don't hesitate to use it.

The addition of curry is ingenious; a perfect seasoning as long as it is not overdone, and here it is used very subtly.

Another nice touch, the sunflower seeds; Enjoy!

Curry Salmon Salad

Serves 6 to 8

INGREDIENTS: *1 ½ cups medium-size shell pasta*
*½ cup of **each**; salted shelled sunflower seeds, finely chopped green pepper, and green onions including tops*
1 cup chopped celery
1 package (10 ounce) frozen peas, thawed and well drained
1 can (7 to 8 ounce) salmon, skin and bones removed, drained (or 8 ounce cooked salmon fillet, skin removed)
3 hard-cooked eggs, thinly sliced
Parsley sprigs, optional garnish
Curry dressing:
¾ cup mayonnaise
1 ½ tablespoons curry powder
1½ tablespoons prepared mustard
¼ cup lemon juice
5 cloves garlic, finely minced
2 cups shredded sharp cheddar cheese

Stir mayonnaise, curry powder, mustard, lemon juice, and garlic together until well blended; stir in cheese.

Cook macaroni according to package directions; rinse and drain.

Prepare curry dressing and set aside.

In a large bowl, combine sunflower seeds, green pepper, onions, celery, peas, and macaroni; pour dressing in and stir until blended; **cover and chill 3 hours or overnight.**

To serve, spoon macaroni mixture onto a large serving platter; flake salmon into the center and garnish with the egg slices.

Optional serving suggestion: Mix flaked salmon into the pasta-curry mixture. Pile onto bed of salad greens. Top with hard-cooked egg slices. (This can be done on individual plates or a large serving platter).

Cobb Salad; Right from Hollywood

I have enjoyed a Cobb salad for years never aware of its interesting origin.

It is said that Mr. Robert Cobb of the Brown Derby restaurant in Los Angeles started it entirely by accident. It was the end of a busy day, and he was scrounging in the iceboxes to see what he could fix quickly and came up with an avocado, some cooked bacon, chicken, tomatoes, lettuce, hard-boiled eggs, and Roquefort cheese. He arranged it all on a plate and the rest is history. I can only guess from there that it was eventually named, placed on the menu and quickly became popular with the customers and celebrities who hung out at the Brown Derby.

My knowledge of this salad is that it is improvised on all the time. When we were traveling through Florida, and stopped to eat, sliced beets and potato salad were included when we ordered their version of the Cobb salad.

I prefer to leave out the bacon, another might not like the blue cheese.

A true Cobb Salad is assembled with the ingredients arranged on the plate in groups.

Start with a bed of romaine lettuce then line up the other ingredients on top. Sometimes watercress and chives are added. The most important element to a good Cobb Salad is the dressing. It should be creamy vinaigrette.

COBB SALAD

Arrange salad greens on individual plates. In rows, arrange portions of sliced cooked chicken, sliced hard-boiled egg, and chunks of tomatoes, cucumber, and avocado. Generously sprinkle on crumbled cooked bacon and blue cheese.

CREAMY VINAIGRETTE

Whisk together 1 teaspoon Dijon mustard, 1 minced clove of garlic, 1/4 teaspoon sugar, 1/2 teaspoon salt, 1/4 teaspoon black pepper, 1 teaspoon Worcestershire sauce, 2 teaspoons lemon juice, 2 tablespoons red wine vinegar, and 1/2 cup extra-virgin olive oil. Mash 1 ounce blue cheese, crumbled, to make a paste and add to dressing when whisking in oil; Spoon over prepared salad.

Undeniably a great summer salad!

TROPICAL CHICKEN SALAD

INGREDIENTS: *5 cups cut-up cooked chicken*
1 can (16 ounce) pineapple chunks, well drained
1 can (8 ounce) sliced water chestnuts, drained

1 cup chopped green pepper
*1 cup **each**; seedless green and red grapes*
1 cup, 4 ounces, shredded Monterey jack cheese or mild
    cheddar
3/4 cup salted cashews
1/2 cup chopped celery
1/2 cup chopped scallions (green onions)
Dressing:
1/3 cup mayonnaise
1/3 cup plain yogurt
4 teaspoons apple juice
Salt and pepper to taste

Combine dressing ingredients, mix well, and set aside. In a large bowl combine all salad ingredients. Add dressing and toss to coat well. Season with salt and pepper; Cover and refrigerate at least 4 hours before serving.

When ready to serve, line a salad platter or bowl with red leaf lettuce (or any lettuce you choose), pile on mixed chicken salad, and enjoy. Makes 8-10 servings

A Selection of Lunch & Side Salads

On many holiday tables serving a salad is a must. If you want something new to try, this salad has all the right ingredients. Fresh spinach leaves or romaine lettuce, are tossed with dried cranberries and toasted walnuts and drizzled with a poppy seed dressing.

CRANBERRY SPINACH SALAD

10 servings

INGREDIENTS: *1 (10 ounce) bag fresh spinach, washed & trimmed (or equal amount romaine lettuce).*
¾ cup dried cranberries
2 green onions sliced
Dressing:
¼ cup sugar
1 teaspoon dried minced onion
¾ teaspoon poppy seeds
Scant ¼ teaspoon paprika
4 tablespoons cider vinegar
¼ cup vegetable oil (canola oil)
¾ cup coarse chopped walnuts, toasted (toast in medium hot, dry non-stick skillet for a few minutes)

In salad bowl, toss greens, cranberries, and onions. In a small bowl, combine spices and poppy seeds.

Whisk in vinegar and oil. Drizzle over salad and sprinkle with walnuts. Toss to coat.

Reader Comment: I have to tell you that the Cranberry-Spinach salad has been a huge hit in my house. When my husband first tasted this salad, he said "finally! A civilized way to eat spinach; this is the only salad you should ever make!" So I do. Regards, Anne P., Haverhill Massachusetts

LEEKS; ENJOY THEIR DELICATE FLAVOR.

Looking a bit like an overgrown green onion, leeks have a sweet flavor all their own. They are similar to onions but much milder. In many parts of the world they are still considered a delicacy, but we have begun to use them as a common ingredient in soups and side dishes, and especially in the classic recipe, "Chilled Leek and Potato soup".

Leeks are delicious raw or cooked. You can add chopped, uncooked leeks to salads, dips, and salsas.

Cooking leeks though will intensify their natural sweetness.

Leeks are more and more available to us year-round, though they are known to be an early spring crop. When buying, look for slender, straight, dry leeks. The bulb should be a bright white, middle section a light green and very tops a darker green. The edible section is the light green and white. The best storage tip is to wrap them in damp paper towels in a plastic bag in your crisper drawer for no more than 5 or 6 days. Wash, trim and separate the leaves just before using.

In this recipe leeks are paired with another spring vegetable, incomparable asparagus.

WARM LEEK, ASPARAGUS AND POTATO SALAD

INGREDIENTS: *2 tablespoons Dijon mustard*
1 tablespoon red wine vinegar
¼ cup canola oil
Salt and freshly ground black pepper to taste
¾ pound fingerling potatoes (or small red-skin potatoes)
1 pound asparagus, cut into 2-inch lengths

2 medium leeks, white and tender green parts, split
lengthwise and cut crosswise into 1 inch pieces
¼ cup snipped chives

In a large bowl, whisk mustard with vinegar. Whisk in oil in a thin stream and season with salt and pepper.

Boil 2 saucepans of salted water. Add potatoes to one, cook for 20 minutes. Cook asparagus and leeks in the other pan for 5 minutes; drain, pat dry and add to the dressing. Drain potatoes, slice half -inch thick and add to bowl.

Add chives, season with salt and pepper and gently toss. Serve warm. Serves 5-6

SUGAR SNAP PEA AND CHERRY TOMATO PASTA SALAD

(4-5 servings)

1. Bring a large pot of salted water to a boil for cooking 8 ounces bowtie pasta, al dente

2. Meantime, make dressing.

INGREDIENTS: *1/2 cup cottage cheese*
1/2 cup buttermilk
1 tablespoon olive oil
2 tablespoons dill (fresh is best, but 2 teaspoons dried
dill can be used)
2 tablespoons fresh or dried parsley
2 and 1/2 tablespoons grated parmesan cheese
1 teaspoon grated lemon lest
1 teaspoon lemon juice

Salt and pepper to taste

In a blender or mini food processor puree cottage cheese until smooth. Add buttermilk and oil; process till smooth. Scrape into a storage container and stir in remainder of ingredients. Cover and refrigerate.

Cook, drain and cool pasta

Cook about a half-pound of fresh sugar snap peas in salted boiling water for no more than 60 seconds, so that they remain crisp-tender. Rinse under cold water and drain well. Place pasta and sugar snaps in a large container and toss with 2 cups of red and yellow cherry tomatoes that you have halved. Add 4 chopped scallions.

Just before serving toss with dressing. (The dressing and salad will keep in a refrigerator or cooler up to 8 hours)

ASPARAGUS & PASTA SALAD WITH ORANGE AND MINT

INGREDIENTS: *8 ounces dry medium pasta shells*
1 pound fresh asparagus, cleaned and cut in 1 inch pieces
½ cup thinly sliced green onions (about 4)
1/3 cup chopped fresh mint
1/3 cup crumbled feta cheese
3 large naval or blood oranges

Cook pasta according to package directions, adding the asparagus the last few minutes of cooking. Drain all; rinse with cold water. Drain; transfer pasta and asparagus to a large serving bowl. Add green onions, mint, and feta cheese to pasta.

With a serrated knife, remove peel and white pith from 2 of the oranges; halve oranges lengthwise, and then slice crosswise. Add to pasta mixture.

Dressing:

From the remaining orange, zest or shred 2 teaspoons peel.

In a covered shaker add 2 tablespoons of the orange juice.

Add: orange peel, 2 tablespoons olive oil, 1 tablespoon white wine vinegar or cider vinegar, ½ teaspoon of each; salt and pepper. Cover and shake well. Pour over pasta mixture; toss to combine.

Refrigerate for one hour before serving to allow flavors to meld. Toss before serving, Makes 8-10 servings.

Fruit Highlight these Side Salads

Known as the "Wedding Salad" as it was first enjoyed at a wedding, with guests impressed with the simple combination of only four ingredients, and how delicious it was.

The dressing chosen for this salad was a creamy sweet onion and perfectly complemented the apples and walnuts.

I make it often and have passed the recipe on to many, many people.

Apple-Walnut Salad

(4 ingredients) OR "Wedding Salad"

INGREDIENTS: *Baby spinach leaves (I substitute with romaine lettuce).
Thinly sliced green apple (peel on)*

Dried cranberries
Coarsely chunked walnuts, toasted. (Toast walnuts in a
*   dry non-stick pan over medium hot heat about 5-7*
*   minutes. Shake pan often so they don't burn).*

There is no actual recipe for the salad, just start with the amount of lettuce you need, sprinkle on a few dried cranberries. Arrange slices of green apple on top, and then sprinkle with toasted walnuts.

If making in a bowl for a number of people, slice apples and add to the greens and cranberries at the last moment as they turn brown quickly (even when sprinkled with lemon juice). Toss with dressing. Add toasted walnuts when ready to serve.

This salad is also good with creamy tarragon, ranch dressing, or sweet onion dressing.

CREAMY TARRAGON DRESSING

INGREDIENTS: *½ cup sour cream*
½ cup mayonnaise
2 teaspoons lemon juice
1 teaspoon onion powder
¼ teaspoon salt
¼ teaspoon pepper
1 teaspoon tarragon leaves, rubbed (When adding, rub
*   between your fingers to release oils)*

Blend all ingredients well. Chill at least 2 hours before serving.

Makes 1 cup, Refrigerate in a tightly covered container up to 2 weeks

Dressing is also good with following combinations, served over lettuce leaves:

Sliced bananas and pineapple chunks

Chicken chunks, celery, and seedless grapes

AVOCADO SALAD WITH HONEYDEW & FONTINA MAKES 4 INDIVIDUAL SALADS

INGREDIENTS: *Large handful of radicchio*

Large handful of any green leaf lettuce such as romaine or arugula

Several slices honeydew melon

2 ripe avocados; peeled and halved, brushed with lemon juice

6 ounces Fontina cheese, cut into small bite-size pieces

DRESSING: *5 tablespoons extra virgin olive oil*

1 tablespoon white wine vinegar

1 tablespoon lemon juice

1 tablespoon chopped fresh parsley

In a small bowl, mix all dressing ingredients. Or shake in a small shaker.

Arrange lettuces on serving plates. Arrange slices of melon over lettuce. Slice each avocado half, place over melon. Top with pieces of cheese (each salad will have about 1 ½ ounces of cheese); Drizzle dressing over all.

SALAD GREENS WITH STRAWBERRIES AND GOAT CHEESE

INGREDIENTS: *6 cups greens; combination of spinach, watercress, romaine is a suggestion*
2 ½ cups sliced fresh strawberries
1/3 cup fresh chives cut into small pieces
½ cup toasted pecans
¼ cup crumbled goat cheese

Dressing: Whisk 1 tablespoon pure maple syrup, 2 tablespoons red-wine vinegar, 1 tablespoon olive oil, 1/4 teaspoon salt, and black pepper to taste in a large bowl;

Add greens, berries, and chives; toss to coat. Divide salad among 4 plates and top with pecans and crumbled cheese.

CITRUS SALAD

Serves 4

INGREDIENTS: *4 cups torn romaine lettuce*
1 avocado, peeled and thinly sliced
½ red onion, thinly sliced
2 oranges, sectioned

DRESSING   *¼ cup olive oil*
½ teaspoon each; lemon and lime peel
1 tablespoon sugar
1 tablespoon lime juice

2 teaspoons orange juice

TOPPING: *In a small skillet toast ¼ cup pecans with 1 tablespoon sugar over low heat, stirring constantly until sugar is melted and pecans coated. Cool and break apart.*

Combine all salad ingredients in serving bowl.

Combine dressing ingredients in a jar and shake until well blended.

When ready to serve toss dressing and salad gently. Sprinkle sugared pecans onto each individual salad.

Comment and request from *Jay: You had a lovely light salad with citrus in it, and in the dressing, in one of your columns; I cannot find the clipping now and am having a dinner for people who cannot eat certain foods, and I believe that salad would be just right. Can you e-mail me a copy? Your recipes inspire me. Thank you.*

Homemade salad dressings provide a fresher taste and have much less sodium and sugar. Keep in a tightly covered glass jar and they keep for 2-3 weeks in your refrigerator.

Note: When making salad dressings in a large batch, seasonings may have to be adjusted. Start with less and add more to your taste.

Often, I do not add salt at all, but pass the salt shaker when serving. Supposedly, less salt is used this way, but you will have to try for yourself.

HOMEMADE RANCH DRESSING

In a medium bowl combine:

1/3 cup plain low-fat yogurt
1 teaspoon Dijon mustard

1 teaspoon white wine vinegar
1 teaspoon honey
Season to taste with coarse salt and ground pepper

VINAIGRETTE WITH CUMIN AND FRESH MINT

Makes 2 cups

1 cup white wine vinegar
3 tablespoons Dijon mustard
4 garlic cloves, finely minced
3 teaspoons ground cumin
Salt to taste
1 teaspoon fresh ground black pepper
1 cup olive oil
*Finely chopped flat-leaf parsley (4 tablespoons fresh, or
    4 teaspoons dried)*
*Finely chopped mint (4 tablespoons fresh or 4 teaspoons
    dried)*

Whisk vinegar, mustard, garlic, cumin and pepper till blended. Slowly add olive oil while whisking; mix well. Add parsley and mint.

BASIC LEMON VINAIGRETTE

¼ cup fresh lemon juice

¼ cup white-wine vinegar
*2 teaspoons sugar (I have not tried this with honey, but
    I suspect it would be good.)*
1 teaspoon coarse salt
¼ teaspoon black pepper

1 cup olive oil

Combine all except oil; whisk or shake till salt and sugar dissolved. Whisk in oil slowly.

Makes 1½ cups; refrigerate up to 2 weeks.

Good with one of these quick salads:

1. Salad greens, kalamata olives and thinly sliced scallions.

2. Radicchio and raisins (pretty with golden raisins).

BALSAMIC VINEGAR

Balsamic vinegar; yes a vinegar yet rich, slightly sweet. I love it, and find it hard to believe that it has been enjoyed in Italy for such a long time, while being fairly new (about 20 years) to American cooks.

Balsamic vinegar has become a pantry essential as it is well suited for vinaigrettes. But in the past several years cooks have looked outside the salad bowl and found it delicious in marinades, glazes for meats and vegetables when grilling, and in sauces.

True balsamic can be very costly indeed; I saw one bottle priced at $50 in the supermarket, and on the internet I have seen prices as high as $200 a bottle. This of course is the real deal; juice of aged Trebbiano grapes, aged in barrels for twelve to twenty-five years, usually from Modeno in Northern Italy.

For your everyday use, look for bottles labeled "Aceto Balsamico di Modena" at supermarkets.

For a treat, look for a small bottle of higher-grade balsamic (marked "condimento" or "tradizionale") from a specialty shop or Italian market

This is a quick-to-make salad dressing that doubles as a marinade.

BALSAMIC-ROSEMARY VINAIGRETTE

In a blender, combine:

> *1/3 cup balsamic vinegar*
> *1 tablespoon Dijon mustard*
> *1 small garlic clove*
> *1 tablespoon fresh rosemary leaves (or ¼ teaspoon dried)*
> *2 tablespoons water*
> *½ teaspoon salt*
> *¼ teaspoon pepper*

Blend above ingredients until smooth. With blender running, add ½ cup extra-virgin olive oil in a thin stream; blend until creamy; Makes ¾ cup; store in refrigerator up to 2 weeks.

CHAPTER 8
INTRODUCTION;
FOOD GIFT IDEAS

Gifts from Your Kitchen

Pecan Date Cheese Ball
Fruit & Nut Brittle
Fudge; Turtle-Cashew & Rocky Road
Chinese Fried Walnuts
Peppermint Snowballs
Homemade Snickers candy
Spiced Pecans
Fruit & Oats Granola

Food Gift Ideas for Homemade Presents

Homemade gifts are special, adding a personal touch and coming right from your kitchen, and usually joyously received. Putting together a homemade food gift can be as easy as mixing together a few items such as a pancake mix and a bottle of real maple syrup with a fancy hot chocolate mix. Try to personalize your gift to the person or family. Teenagers love monster cookies. Someone who loves to cook would love a tin of homemade spice rub. Candied or spiced nuts are perfect for co-workers. For candy lovers make something special like a Fruit & nut brittle, peppermint bark, or decadent homemade snickers (recipe below) that have wowed my family and friends for years. A popular gift I made for my neighbors was a basket that contained a homemade walnut-cheddar cheese ball and a sleeve of crackers with an attached cheese spreader, all prettily wrapped with the recipe attached.

My neighbor Joanne looked forward to that each Christmas.

Once you have made all your gifts, be creative with your packaging. Use jars, tins, or boxes. I have seen wonderful ideas for packing my gifts at the Paper Store and Michaels's Craft store, such as already decorated "chinese food" boxes that make festive and easy containers for many things. Finish everything off with a ribbon or bow and don't forget to include a copy of the recipe if it is a homemade item.

This lightly sweet cheese ball is very creamy and nice to keep on hand for the holidays. You can make it up to 10 days ahead, keeping it tightly wrapped in the refrigerator. It makes a great hostess gift.

(I have wrapped the cheese ball in tissue paper, tied with a ribbon, and placed in a small basket with a couple sleeves of crackers and a cheese-spreader knife. Attach copy of recipe).

Pecan-Date Cheese Ball

INGREDIENTS: *1 teaspoon ground dried mustard*
1 teaspoon water
2 packages (8 ounce each) cream cheese, softened
1/4 cup mayonnaise
1/4 teaspoon ground nutmeg
2 cups sharp cheddar cheese, finely shredded
3/4 cup finely chopped dates
1 cup chopped pecans

In a small bowl, dissolve the mustard in water; let stand for 10 minutes.

In a mixing bowl, beat cream cheese and mayonnaise until smooth. Add nutmeg and mustard mixture. Stir in cheese and dates. Chill for at least 15 minutes. Shape into 2 or 3 balls and roll in pecans till well covered. Wrap tightly in plastic wrap, keep refrigerated. Remove 20 minutes before serving to develop flavor. Serve with choice of crackers. Makes 3 1/2 cups

Reader's Comments:

I wanted to tell you that I made the Pecan-date cheese ball for Thanksgiving and it was a big hit. I made it again today for a party and did not have any dry mustard. I substituted with a scant teaspoon of Dijon mustard and it tastes great; a little more bite but it contrasts nicely with the slight sweetness.

Thanks, **Shelly W.**

I made your recipe for the Pecan-Date Cheese Ball. You suggested that it would make a nice gift. We were invited to my husband's boss's house for dinner, so I made that to bring along with a basket of crackers. There were other guests there and that cheese ball was a big hit. I am not a very good cook, so that made me feel so good.

My husband was shocked (and happy). Thank you for the recipe. **Belinda, North Andover Massachusetts**

This eye-popping confection is a combination of candied fruit, raisins, coconut and a variety of nuts, all of your choice, embedded in a clear brittle and when cool broken into pieces; Surprisingly easy to make.

Fruit & Nut Brittle

Makes about 1 pound candy

INGREDIENTS: *1 ½ cups sugar*
1 cup light corn syrup
4 tablespoons water
14 ounces mixed dried fruit, candied orange or grape-
fruit peel, nuts, raisins, coconut
1 cup candied cherries
2 tablespoons butter
1 teaspoon vanilla extract

Using a heavy saucepan, combine sugar, corn syrup and water; Stir over medium heat until sugar is dissolved.

Using a candy thermometer, cook syrup <u>without stirring</u> until temperature reaches 285 degrees F, or the soft-crack stage.

Add nuts, fruit, candied cherries, butter and vanilla, <u>stirring rapidly</u> until well coated. Quickly spread mixture into a generously buttered 15 inch baking pan (do not use glass). Smooth surface with back of a wooden spoon.

Cool on rack. Remove from pan with a spatula. Break the brittle into pieces and store in an airtight container.

Note: This candy is best made on a cool, low humidity day.

Make Fudge Three Ways for your Gift Giving

The Christmas fairs are in full swing, the dates have been set for office and school parties, cookie and candy swaps, and many other holiday gatherings of all sorts. That means plenty of baking and cooking to keep up with it all.

Using this basic fudge recipe, you can make three kinds of fudge for entertaining or gift giving. With minor substitutions you can make Turtle Cashew Fudge, which is truly delectable....and Rocky Road Fudge, which is very popular with children and teens. And I always made a batch without nuts for school functions.

This recipe is easy to make and stays satin-textured. I spend one day of a weekend and make enough batches of each for all my gift-giving and party needs. It also mails beautifully, and stores well when tightly covered in a cool place.

BASIC FUDGE RECIPE

Makes about 2 and 1/2 pounds fudge or approx. 36 squares

INGREDIENTS: *2 and 1/2 cups sugar*
1/2 cup butter
2/3 cup evaporated milk (5 ounce can)
2 cups marshmallow crème (7 ounce jar)
2 cups chocolate chips (semi-sweet or milk chocolate)
3/4 cup chopped walnuts
1 teaspoon vanilla

Line a 9 inch square pan with foil so that foil extends over sides of pan; butter foil. In large saucepan, combine sugar, butter and milk. Bring to a boil, stirring constantly. Continue boiling 5 minutes over medium heat, stirring constantly. Remove from heat. Add marshmallow and chocolate chips; blend until smooth. Stir in walnuts and vanilla. Pour into prepared pan. Cool to room temperature. Score fudge into 36 squares, or size you wish. Refrigerate until firm. Remove fudge from pan by lifting foil. Remove foil from fudge, and put on cutting surface. Using a very sharp knife, cut through scored lines; Store in refrigerator.

Turtle Cashew Fudge - Substitute cashews for walnuts; 3/4 cup chopped cashews. Stir in 24 caramels, quartered, with cashews and vanilla. Pour into pan. Cool to room temperature; do not refrigerate before cutting. Continue as directed above. In a small microwave container, melt 1/4 of a 14 ounce package of caramels with a tablespoon of whipping cream, light cream, or half & half. Dip the bottom half of a whole cashew in the melted caramel and top each piece of fudge, or spoon a small amount of melted caramel on each fudge piece and top with a whole cashew,

(whichever you find easier).

Fudge should be stored in refrigerator, but served at room temperature so that caramel softens.

Rocky Road Fudge - Stir in 2 cups miniature marshmallows after walnuts and vanilla (marshmallows should not melt completely). Quickly spread in prepared pan.

CHINESE FRIED WALNUTS

This recipe is a little different; a slightly sweet n salty snack that once you start eating you can't put them down.

This recipe was given to me by Mike, my sister's significant other. His sister shared it with him (as well as a gift of the fried walnuts). Mike says she discovered the recipe from a Korean Church group in Pennsylvania. Apparently it was used in a very successful fundraiser. That is the way it goes with good recipes; passed on and passed on.

I suggest filling a pint jar with the finished walnuts, tightly cover, and wrap with a festive ribbon. Don't forget to attach the recipe.

INGREDIENTS: *6 cups water*
4 cups walnuts
1/2 cup sugar
salad oil
salt

Need slotted spoon and thermometer for heating oil; can be made up to 2 weeks ahead.

In a 4 quart pan heat water to boiling. Add walnuts and bring to a boil. Cook 1 minute. Rinse walnuts under hot water. Wash and dry pan well.

In a large bowl with rubber spatula gently stir warm walnuts with sugar until sugar is dissolved. If needed, let mixture stand 5 minutes to dissolve sugar.

Meanwhile, in same pan over medium heat, heat about 1 inch of oil to 350 degrees. With slotted spoon, add about 1/2 walnuts to oil. Fry no more than 5 minutes or until golden brown, (I find that 3 to 4 minutes is best).

Stir often. Be Careful, walnuts will burn quickly.

With slotted spoon, place walnuts in coarse sieve or strainer, over a bowl to drain. Sprinkle very lightly with salt. Taste, adding more salt if needed. The salt taste increases as the walnuts cool. If you want a more sugary taste, add more sugar at this time. Toss lightly to keep walnuts from sticking together. Transfer to paper towels to cool. Continue frying remaining walnuts. _____

Peppermint snowball cookies are so festive and delicious. For gift giving put them in different size chinese food boxes, with red tissue and a candy cane tied to the outside.

Wait until you smell a batch of these cookies baking in your oven!

PEPPERMINT SNOWBALLS

Makes 4 dozen

INGREDIENTS: *1 cup butter, softened*
½ cup confectioners' sugar
1 teaspoon vanilla extract
2 ½ cups all-purpose flour
½ cup ground walnuts or pecans, optional
FILLING: *2 tablespoons cream cheese, softened*
½ cup confectioners' sugar
1 teaspoon milk
3 tablespoons finely crushed peppermint candy
1 drop red food coloring
TOPPING: *½ cup crushed peppermint candy*
½ cup confectioners' sugar

1. In a mixing bowl, cream butter and sugar. Beat in vanilla. Gradually add flour. Stir in nuts. Knead dough until pliable. Cover and refrigerate for 1 hour or until easy to handle.

2. In a small mixing bowl, beat cream cheese, sugar, milk, candy, and food coloring. Roll tablespoonfuls of dough into balls. Using the end of a wooden spoon handle, make a deep indentation in the center of each. Fill with one-quarter teaspoon filling. Cover with one-quarter teaspoonfuls of dough; seal and reshape into balls.

3. Combine topping ingredients; roll balls in topping. Place 1 inch apart on ungreased baking sheets (I like to line baking sheet with parchment paper).

Bake at 350 degrees for 12-14 minutes or until firm. Roll slightly warm cookies in topping again; cool on wire racks.

I have been making homemade snickers since 1996 when I was looking for a new candy recipe to make for gift giving. What followed were so many requests for the recipe it became a tradition. If you make this for gift-giving, I suggest you use one-layer plastic containers with covers (I put in about a dozen good-size pieces), wrapped prettily with a big bow. This makes it convenient for the recipient to keep in the refrigerator. Because this is a popular gift with the guys, I wrap theirs with plain brown paper and tie with raffia.

HOMEMADE SNICKERS CANDY

BOTTOM LAYER: *1 ¼ cups milk chocolate chips (substituting semi-sweet does not give the "snickers flavor")*
¼ cup creamy peanut butter
Filling: 1/4 cup butter
1 cup sugar
¼ cup evaporated milk
1 ½ cups marshmallow crème
¼ cup creamy peanut butter
1 teaspoon vanilla extract
1 ½ cups chopped salted peanuts

CARAMEL LAYER: *1 (14 ounces) package **cooking** caramels (not as soft as snacking caramels)*

¼ cup whipping cream (exact measure)

TOP LAYER: *1 ¼ cups milk chocolate chips*
                        ¼ cup creamy peanut butter

Bottom layer: combine milk chocolate chips and peanut butter in a small saucepan; stir over low heat until melted and smooth. Spread onto the bottom of a lightly buttered 13 inch by 9 inch by 2 inch pan. Refrigerate until set.

Filling: melt butter in a heavy saucepan over medium-high heat. Add sugar and milk. Bring to a boil; boil and stir for 5 minutes. Remove from the heat; stir in the marshmallow crème, peanut butter and vanilla. Add peanuts. Spread over first layer. Refrigerate until set.

Caramel layer: Combine caramels and cream in a saucepan; stir over low heat until melted and smooth. Spread over the filling. Refrigerate until set.

Top layer: Repeat bottom layer by combining milk chocolate chips and peanut butter in a small saucepan; stir over low heat until melted and smooth. Pour over the caramel layer and lightly spread to edges. Refrigerate for several hours, preferably overnight, before cutting. Best when kept refrigerated.

READER'S COMMENT:

I can›t wait to try making the Snickers Candy *Recipe. If it is kept in the refrigerator, how early can I make it?*

Regarding homemade treats, attached is a recipe for chocolate fudge that I have been making for 45 years.

A little about the recipe, my twin grandsons turned 18 recently and I have been making this recipe *with them since they were two years old; one child on one side of me and the other child on the other side, making two batches of fudge (one with nuts and one without). My husband would rescue me when it came time to pour the ingredients from the pan to the prepared casserole dishes. Those are memories that I cherish, especially when the boys recall standing on a chair to stir the fudge and all the silly things that happened in between. True joy if you ask me!*

My husband also makes caramels (from a Betty Crocker book) and pizzelles. Everyone seems to enjoy the homemade treats.

Sharon, Methuen MA

SPICED PECANS

INGREDIENTS: *3 cups pecan halves*
¾ cup sugar
1/3 cup orange juice
2 teaspoons cinnamon
½ teaspoon salt
½ teaspoon ground cloves

Heat oven to 275 degrees. Spread pecans on an ungreased 15x10 inch baking pan. Bake for 10 minutes.

In a medium saucepan, combine sugar, orange juice, and seasonings. Bring to a boil; boil for 2 minutes, stirring occasionally. Remove from heat; stir in nuts.

Using a slotted spoon, remove nuts onto foil or waxed paper. Separate with a fork; let dry. Store in a tight container.

FRUIT & NUT GRANOLA

INGREDIENTS: *2 cups old-fashioned oats (not quick oats or instant)*
1 cup wheaties cereal
1 cup whole almonds or sliced
1 cup pecan halves
1 cup flaked coconut
4 and 1/2 teaspoons wheat germ
1 tablespoon sesame seeds
1/3 cup sunflower seeds
1/2 cup raisins, dried cherries, or dried cranberries
1 teaspoon ground cinnamon

Optional: Toasting the nuts and seeds brings out the flavors. Put nuts and seeds into a dry frying pan that has been heated over medium heat. Lightly toast for a few minutes till lightly browned.

In a large bowl, combine all the above 10 ingredients, mixing to blend cinnamon.

Combine 1/4 cup melted butter, 3 tablespoons honey, and 2 tablespoons real maple syrup; drizzle over oats mixture and stir until well coated.

Pour into a greased 13"x9" baking pan. Bake uncovered at 350 degrees for 30 minutes. Stir every 10 minutes. Cool, and then crumble into pieces.

MORE IDEAS WHEN GIFTS ARE FOOD

1. Have a baking spree with a family member or friend. Set aside two full days or a weekend to "get it all done". Cooking with

someone makes it go fast and is fun. Set up stations. Put on the music and go to it.

2. Try to match gift to recipient such as:

   Energy munch to a family going on a ski trip; Cookie mix to the busy mother down the street; A ready-to-eat (and freeze) entrée for the working couple; Chocolate-covered pretzels or Oreos for the known chocoholics in your family.

3. Include the recipe. This is not only because they may want to make it themselves, but also to insure there are no allergies to the ingredients.

CHAPTER 9
HELP IN THE KITCHEN

MAKE YOUR OWN; RUBS, MARINADES, SPICES, MUSTARD

NEW ORLEANS RUB
BASIC SEASONING SALT
ITALIAN SEASONING
HONEY-THYME MARINADE
ZESTY BEEF MARINADE
MAPLE MUSTARD BASTING SAUCE
HONEY MUSTARD SAUCE
HOMEMADE MUSTARD
GROW FRESH HERBS; FRESH HERB VINAIGRETTE
HOMEMADE BREADCRUMBS
ABOUT MUSHROOMS

BAKING:

APPLE PIE SPICE
PUMPKIN PIE SPICE
TIP: 5-SPICE POWDER AND CINNAMON
TIP: CREAM OF TARTAR
MAKE CRYSTALLIZED GINGER
TIP: SHINY FRUIT GLAZE
TIPS: BAKING COOKIES
ENTERTAINING: CHOCOLATE PLUNGE DIP
SOFT PRETZELS

BENEFITS OF MAKING YOUR OWN.....AND MORE

1. Economical

2. Healthier for you and your family, manage amounts of sugar and salt, or add none.

3. More flavorful than store-bought blends.

4. It doesn't take a lot of time, and you will get lots of compliments.

5. Makes a welcome gift; i.e. give New Orleans Rub at the beginning of summer grilling, give pumpkin pie spice in November prior to the holidays, give an assortment to a new Bride and Groom.

This rub I use for all my grilling, it's great on anything! And it keeps for a year.

NEW ORLEANS RUB

INGREDIENTS: *¼ cup coarse salt (kosher or sea)*

3 tablespoons paprika
2 tablespoons garlic powder
2 tablespoons onion powder
2 tablespoons dried thyme (ground)
2 tablespoons dried oregano
2 tablespoons freshly ground black pepper
2 teaspoons ground dried sage
2 teaspoons cayenne pepper

Combine above seasonings in a small bowl and whisk to mix, or place in jar and shake.

Store in an airtight jar away from direct heat and light; it will keep for at least 1 year.

Basic Seasoning Salt

Use year round on roasted vegetables and to season most everything. Use it to season your meats before marinating. (Keep in a shaker near your stove and grill)

INGREDIENTS: *1 cup coarse salt*
1 tablespoon garlic powder
1 tablespoon and 1 teaspoon ground black pepper

Italian Seasoning

INGREDIENTS: *2 Tablespoons each; Basil, Oregano, Rosemary, Marjoram, Thyme, Dried Parsley*
1 Tablespoon Sage
1 teaspoon granulated garlic (optional)

Mix well and store in airtight jar.

Honey-Thyme Marinade;

Great for chicken, pork, shrimp.

INGREDIENTS: *3 cloves minced garlic*
1/3 cup olive oil
2/3 cup orange juice
¼ cup honey mustard
3 tablespoons honey
¾ teaspoon dried thyme

Mix all ingredients and store in refrigerator. When ready to use put marinade in a gallon-size Ziploc bag, add meat, seal, and let marinate for 4 to 12 hours. Shake off excess when grilling.

Zesty Marinade for Beef

INGREDIENTS: *2/3 cup bottled steak sauce*
6 tablespoons lemon juice
4 tablespoons canola or vegetable oil
1 tablespoon sugar (I start with 1 teaspoon and taste-test)

Mix all together and refrigerate. When using, marinate steaks, kabobs, etc. for at least 4 hours.

Maple Mustard Basting Sauce

INGREDIENTS: *2 tablespoons Dijon mustard*
¼ cup pure maple syrup
1 teaspoon lemon juice

1 teaspoon pepper & pinch salt
1 teaspoon melted butter

Place fillets on pan and brush with butter; coat with maple-mustard sauce. Place under broiler leaving oven door tipped open. Continue to coat with remaining sauce while broiling.

Serve with pan juices spooned over salmon, chicken and other fish when grilling or broiling.

Honey-Mustard Sauce

INGREDIENTS: *1/3 cup Dijon mustard or homemade*
1/3 cup honey
2 tablespoons chopped fresh dill or 1 tablespoon dried dill
1 teaspoon freshly grated orange peel (or 2 tablespoons orange marmalade)

Combine mustard and honey in a small bowl. Stir in the dill and orange; will baste 3-4 pieces of chicken. (Sauce can be made ahead and refrigerated up to 1 week).

Homemade Mustard

This recipe makes **sweet-hot mustard** which keeps indefinitely in the refrigerator, and needs no cooking. This makes one quart and can be halved.

*Colman's Dry Mustard is known as the English mustard and has been around a long time.

INGREDIENTS: *3 cups all-purpose flour*

4 ½ tablespoons *Colman's dry mustard
1 cup white sugar
1 cup brown sugar; loosely packed
1 tablespoon salt

Combine all ingredients. Slowly blend in full strength cider vinegar until desired consistency. Whisk until smooth. Yield- 1 quart

GROW FRESH HERBS IN A MINI HERB GARDEN.

If you cook, you will love having fresh herbs always ready to put into your recipe.

When nights are warmer than forty degrees plant rosemary, thyme, and oregano in a pot that is at least eighteen inches wide. Use a well-draining potting soil, and place the pot outdoors in full sun. Using a waterproof marker, write on a Popsicle stick name of each herb to mark where planted. If you would like to grow mint, it should be in its own pot as it spreads.

Here is basic vinaigrette to make when using your fresh cut herbs.

FRESH HERB VINAIGRETTE

Using an oil & vinegar cruet or jar, fill one-third full of olive oil.

Add an equal amount of your favorite vinegar. Take two, 2-inch sprigs of desired herb such as oregano or thyme and pinch leaves off of stems into the cruet. Some herbs are stronger than others so I would suggest a taste-test in case you need to add more. Add salt & pepper to your liking.

Make Your Own Breadcrumbs

4 slices of bread makes about 1 cup crumbs.

Dry bread in a 300 degree oven for approximately 10-15 minutes; halfway through turn them so they dry evenly. Remove from oven and let cool. Tear dried bread into smaller pieces and place in your food processor or blender; Process until desired coarseness. I grind mine into a coarse texture. This way, if I need finer crumbs, I just regrind the amount needed when making my dish.

Tip-Onion rolls make nicely flavored seasoned breadcrumbs.

About Mushrooms

Shitakes are great for stir-fries. Remove their stems before using. Exotic-looking but relatively easy to cultivate, **Oyster** mushrooms have a pleasant, mild flavor and a soft texture.

Cremini are actually baby versions of **Portobello's**. Both have a bold and meaty flavor.

The old standby, lightly flavored white **or** button mushroom, is mild enough to work well with anything from rosemary to lemongrass.

Baking

For your baking needs make your own spices. These can be very costly when purchased in the store.

APPLE PIE SPICE

> *4 teaspoons ground cinnamon*
> *2 teaspoons nutmeg*
> *1 teaspoon cardamom*

PUMPKIN PIE SPICE

> *4 teaspoons ground cinnamon*
> *2 teaspoons ground ginger*
> *1 teaspoon ground allspice*
> *1 teaspoon ground nutmeg*

Store spices in airtight screw-top jars in a cool dark place in your cupboard.

INTERCHANGEABLE; 5-SPICE POWDER & CINNAMON

Tip courtesy Pat from Andover, MA

"You can buy 5- spice powder at most any grocery store. It consists of cinnamon, anise, fennel, ginger, and cloves. It has the most wonderful aroma and is used in Chinese cooking. The first time I bought it, the store cashier told me she uses it in her apple pies instead of cinnamon and nutmeg!

I just made a batch of Apple Squares this morning using the 5-spice and I had an afterthought: wouldn't they be delicious with caramel drizzled over the top?"   Pat, Andover MA

Cook's tip: Cream of tartar is most commonly used to beat egg whites in meringues, cookies, and cake recipes.

If you don't do a lot of baking you probably don't have it.

You can substitute 2 teaspoons of white vinegar or lemon juice for 1 teaspoon of cream of tartar.

Crystallized ginger; Here is an easy recipe. First, slice one-half cup fresh ginger. Next, boil sugar-water (1 cup sugar to 2 cups water) and sliced ginger for at least 1 hour or until the mixture becomes translucent. Remove the ginger from the sugar syrup, and cool it completely. Roll the ginger in granulated sugar; store in an airtight container. It's a good idea to do this a month ahead of your holiday cooking to save time.

Ginger is known for its distinct aroma and adds a warm hint of spice to any recipe. Found in the produce section, fresh ginger is firm with smooth skin. It is simple to peel using a vegetable peeler. Cut off what you need and the rest will keep in your fridge for weeks.

Reader's comment: *I am making cupcakes filled with ricotta cheese and would like to know how to have fresh fruit such as strawberries, raspberries, & blueberries look shiny when topping off cupcakes. I am doing this for a bridal shower and would appreciate your suggestions. Many thanks, Carol*

Cook's Tip: For strawberries and raspberries, melt down strawberry jelly in a small saucepan. Let cool to room temp and gently brush on a light coat. This gives a shiny, rosy blush.

For fruits such as pineapple, blueberries and kiwi, use clear apple jelly, melted and cooled a bit.

Tips when baking cookies:

1. Line cookie sheet with parchment paper instead of greasing it. Fewer cleanups.

2. Cookies darken too fast when baked in the lower third of oven. If you are making several batches and need to do this, put cookies on 2 cookie sheets stacked together.

3. If you prefer soft cookies, slightly under bake them; pale in center with golden brown edges.

4. Don't over mix cookie dough or brownie batter once dry ingredients have been added; this will overdevelop the gluten, making less tender and change the texture.

5. When adding raisins or other dried fruits to cookie dough, "plump" first by letting them soak in boiling water for a couple of minutes. Drain well.

ENTERTAINING

Chocolate Plunge, a chocolate dip served warm.

To make 1 ½ cups, you will need 2/3 cup light corn syrup, 1/2 cup whipping cream, and 8 ounces semi-sweet chocolate. Microwave the syrup and cream in a medium size bowl on HIGH about 1 ½ minutes or until mixture comes to a boil; stir in chocolate till completely melted.

Great served with Biscotti, pretzels, large marshmallows, and strawberries. This is especially nice with champagne.

Reader's comment:

Your recipe for "chocolate plunge", the dipping sauce, made New Year's a lot of fun. It was different and raved about by my friends. You have great ideas and your recipes are easy. Vicky, Atkinson, NH

Soft Pretzel Round

A soft pretzel made quick by using refrigerated soft breadsticks that you buy in the supermarket.

INGREDIENTS: *11 ounce can refrigerated pre-made soft breadsticks*
1 egg
coarse salt

Preheat oven to 350 degrees. Lightly butter a cookie sheet. Separate breadsticks into 8 pieces. Unroll and shape each stick into a 15 inch rope; form into a pretzel. Arrange pretzels side by side on a baking sheet to form a 10 inch circle. Lightly brush with beaten egg. Sprinkle with coarse salt (also may use sesame seeds if desired).

Bake 15 to 18 minutes until golden brown. Serve warm with mustard-butter.

Mustard-Butter: In a small bowl mix 1/2 cup unsalted softened butter with 2 tablespoons Dijon mustard. Beat till fluffy.

Olive-Nut Spread

Nearly ten years ago a national woman's magazine published their most requested recipes since their first edition. This recipe was first published in their magazine in 1952, and was not only the most requested recipe of that year, but also the most requested in the history of the magazine. I found that interesting so I began making it for parties and get-togethers, and it is well liked, especially so for those who love green olives.

I prefer to serve this spread on plain, buttery crackers.

INGREDIENTS: *6 ounces cream cheese, softened*
1/2 cup mayonnaise

1 cup green salad olives, finely chopped (save juice)
dash black pepper
1/2 cup finely chopped pecans or walnuts

Mix softened cream cheese and mayonnaise. Add 2 tablespoons juice from the olives, dash of pepper, mix well. Fold in nuts and olives. Chill for at least 2 hours before serving to blend flavors. Serve with your favorite crackers.

IMITATION BOURSIN CHEESE SPREAD

INGREDIENTS: *2 packages (8 ounce each) cream cheese at room temperature*
2 sticks (4 ounce each) butter at room temperature
*2 cloves garlic, **finely** minced*
*½ teaspoon of **each** seasoning:*
dried thyme, dried basil, dried marjoram, dried dill weed, fresh black pepper

Mix all ingredients together by hand in a large bowl; after blending shape ingredients into a ball.

Tightly wrap and refrigerate for 24 hours to allow flavors to blend.

Let ball come to room temperature before serving. Serve with assorted crackers

Try Boursin spread on bagels, slathered onto a grilled steak, or mixed into scrambled eggs.

QUICK & EASY DIP

INGREDIENTS: *8 ounce cream cheese, softened*
                1 cup shredded cheddar cheese
                1 cup any chunky salsa

Spread cream cheese in a 9" microwavable pie plate. Sprinkle on cheddar cheese. Microwave about 2 minutes until cheese is melted (or melt in oven).

Top with Salsa. Serve with Tortilla chips.

BEVERAGES

CAFE' OLE'

Serve this rich hot coffee that combines cinnamon and chocolate.

To make 1 serving, spoon 2 tablespoons of a coffee-flavored liqueur and 1 tablespoon instant cocoa mix into a mug. Fill with hot, strong coffee; stir well to blend. Garnish with a dollop of whipped cream and a cinnamon stick.

MOCHA JAVA ICE CREAM SHAKE

(makes 2 cups)

Place ½ cup cold, brewed, very strong coffee in a blender.

Place ½ of a milk-chocolate candy bar with almonds in blender, broken into a few large pieces. Frozen snickers good too. (Any candy bar of your choice)

Blend till candy is in small pieces.

Add 2 cups of coffee, chocolate, or vanilla ice cream; cover and blend till smooth.

Pour into glass, top with whipped cream and serve immediately.

POMEGRANATE TEA

(makes four, 8 ounce cups)

INGREDIENTS: *3 cups water*
3 tablespoons sugar
4 regular size black tea bags
1 cup pomegranate juice
¼ teaspoon almond extract
Lemon wedges

In a medium saucepan bring water and sugar to a boil, remove from heat. Add tea bags. Let stand for 30 minutes, remove tea bags. Add pomegranate juice and extract.

Tea can be served hot or iced. Serve with a lemon wedge. Sweeten to taste with brown or white sugar.

CRANBERRY RUM PUNCH

(makes 3 or 4 servings)

Combine 1 cup cranberry juice and one-third cup dark rum.

Serve over ice in a short cocktail glass. Run lime wedge around glass rim.

This beverage is as good for a brunch as well as an evening get-together.

Almond milk is very popular with people who prefer not to drink dairy milk. Here is a recipe to make your own should you wish to do so.

ALMOND MILK

1. Soak 16ounces natural almonds in water overnight. Being a live food, this transforms the almond from a carbohydrate to a protein and allows for easier digestion.

2. Put almonds in a blender and fill just over halfway with water. Some people like to add a handful of raw figs to sweeten the milk but others find the milk naturally sweet enough.

3. Blend thoroughly. If too thick, add more water. Look for a light, drinkable texture.

4. Some prefer to strain through a "milk bag" or cheesecloth to separate the pulp, or a finer consistency, but this writer prefers the pulp version. Yields just over one-half gallon.

VEGAN TIPS

- Protein, choose 5 or more servings per day of protein-rich foods like legumes, nuts, seeds, and soy foods.

  A serving is ½ cup cooked beans, 2 tablespoons nut butter or chopped nuts, 1 cup soymilk, or 1 ounce of a meat analog.

- Have a serving of a vitamin C-rich food at every meal. Choose melons, citrus fruits, pineapple, strawberries, kiwifruit, broccoli, peppers, tomatoes, or potatoes. These foods give iron absorption a boost.

- Eat lots of brightly colored vegetables; leafy greens, pumpkin, sweet potatoes, carrots and dark squashes.

- Fortified soymilk and fruit juices are great sources of well-absorbed calcium. You can also get this nutrient from firm tofu made with calcium sulfate, leafy greens like collards, kale and Bok Choy, and from cooked dried beans. Check out rice pasta as an alternative to whole wheat pasta.

READER'S COMMENT:

Sharing the fridge with my vegan kids has opened my world a bit. I actually like soy milk on my cereal, once I found a brand and flavor I liked, some are too sweet. And I am conscientious about planning a meatless meal more often. My kids have told me about fabulous cupcakes made with avocado. I attended a wedding of two vegans in NYC where the most scrumptious chocolate cupcakes were served. I love it all. **Kathy C., Methuen MA**

COUNTDOWN GUIDE FOR HOLIDAY DINNERS

(Helpful if cooking for a crowd)

This guide will help you to remember the many details during this busy time.

For me, it means fewer "To Do" lists taped to my refrigerator.

DAY 6

China, silverware, tablecloth; clean and ready to use.

Clean out refrigerator and freezer, you will need the space.

Make place cards; decide on centerpiece

Day 5

Write shopping list; purchase non-perishables, wines.

Arrange for rented or borrowed chairs if needed.

Day 4

Make pie dough. Form into discs, tightly wrap in plastic and refrigerate in covered container.

If cooking a frozen turkey, pick it up now as defrosting can take up to 3 days in refrigerator depending upon size.

Day 3

If possible, set table now. This frees up time on the Event Day and helps you to have it just the way you would like it.

Assemble serving pieces; gravy bowl, vegetable bowls, platters, spoons, etc.

Buy any remaining ingredients.

If making, prepare cranberry sauce or chutney. Prepare cheese ball.

Prep chopped items; considering your menu & recipes, save time by chopping onions, celery, nuts, and the like, and keeping in tightly covered containers in a cool place.

DAY 2

Finish anything not done from above.

Last minute cleaning

DAY 1

Day before: early in day make pies, or pick up if ordered from bakery.

Peel vegetables such as sweet potatoes, butternut squash, turnip, and keep in cold water in a cool place.

Prepare any dishes that can be cooked today and reheated tomorrow (such as stuffed acorn squash, soups, etc.)

Day of Event Have meat or main dish ready for oven time.

Peel and cut-up potatoes; keep in a pot of cold water.

Prepare appetizers and side vegetables.

Make gravy or sauces if using.

Finally, relax and enjoy the day!

ANNUAL KITCHEN "TO DO" LIST

January is my month to do this. Set whatever time is good for your schedule.

1.   Replace baking supplies.

Over time, moisture accumulates in opened packages of baking powder or soda and can alter the results of your baking. After opening, store cans or boxes in a sealed zip-top plastic bag to keep them fresh longer.

Check spices. Some are dated. Some spices don't have as long a shelf life as others.

Spices don't spoil, they do lose flavor intensity. If the color appears faded, the intensity probably is also.

Shelf-life guidelines:

Ground spices such as nutmeg, cinnamon, turmeric, 2-3 years

Basil, oregano, dried parsley, 1-2 years

Whole spices, 4-5 years

Poppy seeds and sesame seeds, 2 years

2. Check Flours if not used for several months.

You should throw out flour once a year if you don't use it often. Whole wheat or soy flour will keep longer stored in your refrigerator or freezer, because the oil in the flour causes it to become rancid faster than regular flour.

It is important to have cold flours brought to room temperature before using.

It is wise to transfer flour from its paper package to an air-tight opaque container.

3. Check your freezer and toss frozen foods that may have opened or developed serious freezer burn.

CPSIA information can be obtained at www.ICGtesting.com
Printed in the USA
BVOW03s2332110516

447744BV00003B/3/P